I CHING
FOR TEENS

Take Charge of
Your Destiny
with the
Ancient Chinese Oracle

Julie Tallard Johnson

Bindu Books

Rochester, Vermont

Bindu Books
One Park Street
Rochester, Vermont 05767
www.InnerTraditions.com

Bindu Books is a division of Inner Traditions International

Library of Congress Cataloging-in-Publication Data

Johnson, Julie Tallard.
  I ching for teens : take charge of your destiny with the ancient
Chinese oracle / Julie Tallard Johnson.
     p. cm.
  ISBN 978-0-89281-860-0 (pbk.)
  1. Yi jing—Juvenile literature.   I. Title.
  PL2464.Z7 T34 2001
  299'.51282—dc21

                              2001004487

Printed and bound in the United States

10 9 8 7 6 5 4 3 2

Text design and layout by Priscilla Baker
This book was typeset in Benguiat, with Futura and Present as display typefaces

This book is dedicated to the Sage that is within you; that *is* you.

Acknowledgments

I would like to acknowledge my greatest teacher—Adversity. Without it I would still be afraid. And to all the Wisdomkeepers who passed on the love and wisdom of the I Ching.
Thank you George at the General store, and to all like him who offer their ideas as easily as the sun offers light.
Finally, I am grateful to the trees that were used in the making of this book.

Contents

Introduction:
The World According to the I Ching

Oracle: *the place where, or medium by which,*
deities are consulted.
—Webster's New World Dictionary, 2nd edition

The Oracles were the ancient world's combination
of counseling center, holy place, fortune-teller,
opinion shaper, school for prophets, dispenser of
medical and political advice, and point of contact
between the human and the divine.
—Barbara Walker, The Woman's Dictionary of Symbols and Sacred Objects

I am so glad you found your way to this book and to the wisdom of the I Ching. This is because the I Ching has been such a great help to me and I know it can be so for you too. Wonderful changes can take place in your life as a result of consulting the I Ching and applying its wisdom. You have now found a source of help you can rely on your entire life, if you choose. The I Ching, also called the Book of Changes, teaches us that everything—no matter what form it takes (difficult or pleasurable)—holds within it a golden thread of possibility, a possibility to turn things around if they are bad. The I Ching also teaches that everything is changing, nothing remains the same, and true happiness comes from accepting our changing state while living in the present moment.

The answers you receive from the I Ching offer insight into not only what you need for a particular situation but also the *potential* of what could develop. When you use the counsel of the I Ching in a positive way, you can turn a potentially negative situation into a new opportunity. The more you use and think about the I Ching and its meaning, the more you will gain an understanding of its messages.

It is important to approach the I Ching with a sincere and open mind. This sincerity will help you get clear advice, because your mind will be more receptive to the guidance it offers. Asking the I Ching for guidance means you are tapping in to an ancient oracle that will help you take the best path. It allows you to glimpse inside yourself and find answers. The I Ching will challenge you to grow, to be the best human being you can be, and to bring forth your greatest potential in a situation. This is what it has done for me.

History of the I Ching

The I Ching is so old—believed to be at least three thousand years old—that its original intent is somewhat of a mystery. Many scholars attribute the first works of the I Ching to legendary Chinese chieftain Fu Shi. Fu Shi is believed to have taught his people the finer arts of fishing, hunting, and animal husbandry, so many metaphors within the original text refer to these activities. He is credited for creating the sixty-four hexagrams (six-line symbols) on which the I Ching is based.

History suggests that King Wen, who founded the Zhou Dynasty (1150–249 B.C.) in China, expanded a great deal on the oracle, and his son, the Duke of Zhou, completed the book with writings for each of the lines within the hexagrams. Later, Confucius (551–479 B.C.), a well-known Chinese philosopher and scholar, made large contributions to the commentaries about the hexagrams and their individual lines. Carl Jung, the famous Swiss psychologist, helped bring the I Ching to the West in the early 1900s.

Today there are estimated to be thousands of commentaries on the I Ching. Thomas Cleary, a known scholar of East Asia and the I Ching, says, "this continued interest in the I Ching is enhanced by the fact that the book has never been universally regarded as the sole property of any particular religion, cult, or school of thought." The I Ching belongs to all who seek its wisdom.

My version of the I Ching is the first one written for teens and those moving toward independence. In most ancient cultures, the teen years were when one was taught how to consult oracles, such as the I Ching, for guidance. Oracles are a precious resource for teens, guiding us through our teen years and the move into adult independence. Each hexagram in the I Ching speaks to the questions and concerns we all have during our young adult years. Use this book to help you whenever you need more insight or suggestions. Use it when you need a sense of a situation's potential. Use it knowing that it is a source of wisdom that has helped to guide people for thousands of years.

Finding My Way to the I Ching

I began to consult the I Ching at the age of sixteen. Looking back some thirty years, I would say that the I Ching found me as much as I found it. I began smoking pot at the age of twelve. I decided in my sophomore year of high school that it was time to give up my abuse of marijuana and take up meditation. I watched friends and family members be destroyed by alcohol and drugs. I decided it was time to choose my path. I chose to get off the path of drugs and put both feet on the path of Spirit. This choice saved my life. I was in search of something—something greater than my problems. I was in search of myself and my place in the world. And I needed a way to channel the intense questions and energy I carried inside of me.

In my yoga teachings it speaks of not worrying about tomorrow. Well, I am drowning in it! And it creates such unhappiness in me and throws me off balance today. But what about when this tomorrow becomes today, kicking me in the face? I need to think about tomorrow. Dear Self, I know I am too much into proving myself to others around me. I pray peace comes to me. I have faith in myself and in God but this waxes and wanes like the moon. How can I live in the present moment and still plan for my future? Because here it comes, ready or not!

—taken from the author's journal, May 29, 1972, age 16

My search took me to many strange and wonderful places—a southern Baptist congregation in Florida, Aldous Huxley's books, transcendental meditation classes, Quaker Friendship meetings, solitude in nature, yoga classes, Bible classes, A Course in Miracles, volunteer work at a community center, and the Northern Shore in Wisconsin. Finally, after many trips to the library and bookstore, I discovered a small book titled *Essential Changes: The Essence of the I Ching.* I began to consult the I Ching regularly while continuing my meditation and yoga practice. Positive changes began to take shape slowly in my life. I worried less and hung out with others who meditated. I felt freer of what others thought of me; and I attended an alternative high school for my junior and senior years. Increasingly I had a stronger sense of purpose and direction in my life. And each time adversity did strike, I found I had the wisdom and strength to deal with it. Now, I attribute much of my inner strength and happiness, as well as my successes, to the counsel I received from the I Ching. I have found the I Ching to be the most loving of counselors, a guide through difficult times, and a source of continued insight.

Diary of a Mad Student

Dear Self,

I woke up by the sound of a loud and aggressive ring from my alarm clock. It has to go! Shocks all the dreams away. I shut it off and sleep in. But I get myself up to study for tomorrow's exam. Study, study, study. Coffee resurrects me, I meditate for a short time, and then choose the clothes that fit my mood or maybe create a mood—and I am off to classes. Dance class, what a relief. So I can dance dance dance and get credit. I am failing algebra, but who cares? I fail to function properly at the proper time for the proper people. My math T.A. understands me, my French T.A. hates me—I couldn't remember the French word for "rain." I skipped my methods class because I was upset about the quiz I took on Monday.

Will the professor even notice I am not there? I had lunch with a friend who agrees that we take school way too seriously. And we laughed a bit, but by the end of the day I am feeling stupid. I came home and cried. And consulted the I Ching. I ask the I Ching: What of my independence, from school, from men, my relationship to my youth? It replies:

Hexagram 35 changing into 64—#35 Progress: The image is of sun over earth. The superior person polishes bright virtues. Changing line: Apparent progress and sorrow. Be firm and correct and good fortune will result (don't give up on myself). Great blessings from grandmother.

#64 Before Completion: and the image is fire over water. Progress and success (so don't give up—you are almost done with this semester). The great person carefully considers things and places.

—May 1977, journal entry and I Ching consultation

Understanding the I Ching

The I Ching is to be taken seriously. It is an oracle, a Wisdomkeeper that you can rely on and to which you can bring all your concerns. It contains within it wisdom that can help you with the big and small matters of your life. You may simply want to know more of what this particular day or week will bring, or you may need more insight into a particular situation. It will answer your direct question: "How should I choose between going out West or staying home for the summer?" It will also address other issues that are important to you at the time, such as your attitude; your self-esteem; your role in relation to school, family, and friends; and spiritual matters such as having faith and accepting the time it takes for things to happen. You might say that the I Ching's intent is to help you become the best human being possible.

When you consult the I Ching you consult the wisdom contained within the I Ching, and you consult the wisdom contained within yourself. The I Ching is a guide through the inner world of feelings, thoughts, beliefs, and attitudes and the outer world of relationships and events. You can consult the I Ching every day, weekly, or just when you feel you have a pressing issue. When you ask a question daily, the answer will pertain to that day, or that week if you inquire weekly. When you have a particular issue in mind, the hexagram you receive will address that particular question. If the response doesn't quite make sense, or is one that you don't like, try to remain open to what the I Ching is saying to you. Sometimes what we most *need* to hear is not what we *want* to hear! Just consider what it is trying to suggest.

Just as with a spiritual elder or mentor, the I Ching requires your sincerity and trust when you approach it. It is like all relationships—what you bring to it influences what you get out of it. For those of you who consult the I Ching regularly, with a sincere heart, and use the wisdom offered in its readings, you will experience its rewards—insight, happiness, healthier relationships, and greater peace of mind. These rewards will nurture you throughout your teen years and beyond.

The Story behind the Hexagrams

The I Ching is based on the concept of two opposite energies. Originally called the light and the dark, these energies are now referred to as yin and yang. Everything in life is understood to have both light and dark, yin and yang energies.

 Yang represents the masculine, the light energy (like the sun), the Creative principle (the first hexagram).

Yin energy is the feminine, the dark energy (like the soil or womb), the Earth (passive) principle (the second hexagram). All the hexagrams within the I Ching are a combination of these two basic energies of yin and yang.

The interaction of yin and yang (which is constant) is what creates change. Through the I Ching we understand that all things and situations arise from a combination of yin and yang principles. The movement of yin and yang is understood as the movement and expression of the Tao. The Tao is the invisible, unifying principle and energy that connects us all (see hexagram 29). The Tao is always changing, as is our life. Therefore, the I Ching, or Book of Changes, guides us through these changes by being an oracle of change. When we are able to move through life with openness and flexibility, having the ability to move through our life with integrity, true happiness results.

Each hexagram, or gua, originates from the two energies of yin and yang. The I Ching is based on the belief that all things and situations arise from a combination of yin and yang energies: light and dark, masculine and feminine, soft and hard. And that every situation is in a state of change—that a difficult situation contains the potential to become positive, just as a positive situation has the potential to become negative. Each hexagram gives us more insight into the underlying Tao present in each situation and what we might do to best respond to the concern at hand. Each hexagram is made up of two trigrams; the trigrams are the yin or yang energy contained within the reading (see Identifying Your Hexagram on page 226).

 Earth above (yin)

Heaven below (yang)

Where the yin or yang energy is placed (above or below) gives us a certain hexagram: earth above, heaven below gives us hexagram #11 with the image of "heaven on earth." Each hexagram, and the placement of the lines, represent movement from one state to another. Each line and its placement then holds significance. (For more on understanding the Tao of the I Ching and its images refer to the bibliography on page 225.)

How to Consult the I Ching

Preparation: Give yourself a good half hour to consult the I Ching. Have three pennies or three I Ching coins, available at bead stores and new age markets. Although we now use coins, sticks, and cards, the people who first consulted the I Ching used bones! You can also make your own objects for consulting the I Ching. See the box on page 9 for some ideas on this. Read through all the steps once carefully and look over the hexagrams on page 226 to familiarize yourself with how to identify them. Do a couple practice tosses before you begin to consult the I Ching, so you can get comfortable with using and counting/reading the coins. After doing this a few times, you will know the steps and will no longer need to refer to these instructions.

Step one: Formulate the question or concern that you want help with. This could be a specific issue that concerns you, a decision you are trying to make, something you are ready to change but want advice on, or a problem you want to resolve. You may want to keep a journal to write the question/concern down in and then record the translation you receive from the I Ching. It is helpful to look back over the weeks or months to see what was concerning you and how the I Ching responded to your inquiries.

Step two: As you toss the coins, focus on your issue or question. Also pay attention to other concerns and thoughts that arise in your mind as you consult the I Ching. If you find yourself thinking a lot about a certain person or concern, there is a good chance that the I Ching will address this in its answer as well.

Toss the coins six times. Heads count as 3 and tails count as 2. The I Ching coins have heads and tails as well. When you toss the coins, write out the numbers starting with the bottom line first. Remember to proceed up from the first line, not down. Your toss may look like this:

Sixth line: (2 heads and 1 tail)	8
Fifth line: (3 heads)	9
Fourth line: (1 head and 2 tails)	7
Third line: (3 tails)	6
Second line: (1 head and 2 tails)	7
First line: (2 heads and 1 tail)	8

If you make a mistake in your math, don't worry, just continue with the numbers and the hexagram they create. Trust that this is the message that you were meant to receive.

Step three: Place the corresponding lines next to the numbers. All even numbers are broken lines; odd numbers are solid lines. So the above example will look like this:

```
 8   ———   ———
*9   ———   ———
 7   ———————
*6   ———   ———
 7   ———————
 8   ———   ———
```

Step four: Identify the changing lines (identified here by asterisks). All sixes and nines are changing lines. What this means is that they change into their opposite—solid lines become broken lines, and broken lines become solid. This then creates a second hexagram. If there are no sixes or nines, then you have no changing lines and therefore no second hexagram.

```
 8   ———   ———        8   ———   ———
*9   ———————         *9   ———   ———
 7   ———————          7   ———————
*6   ———   ———       *6   ———————
 7   ———————          7   ———————
 8   ———   ———        8   ———   ———
```

First Hexagram (#47)   Second Hexagram (#32)

Step five: Now that you have your hexagrams drawn out, match them up with the diagram on page 226. Match the bottom 3 lines (trigram) with the top three lines (trigram) to come up with your hexagram. The number on the chart that lies at their intersection indicates which hexagram you have thrown. There are sixty-four possibilities.

Step six: Find the page in the book of the given hexagram and read the main hexagram description. If you have changing lines, read the entry for those specific lines as well. In the above example you would read the main entry for hexagram 47 and also lines 3 and 5 (from the bottom up). Then you would read the second hexagram main text description, which in this case is hexagram 32. You do not read the individual lines in a second hexagram, only the main text.

Changing Lines and Second Hexagrams

Changing lines, also known as moving lines, hold special significance because they are offering you more specific insight into your issue or question. Read the main text of the hexagram first, and then the changing lines only for those lines that are sixes and nines. When you do receive changing lines, you read the changing lines only for the first hexagram, not the second hexagram.

The second hexagram can be understood as giving you more insight into your question, and it may also reflect the potential of the situation. The potential of a given situation is what might develop depending on how you respond to the I Ching's counsel and what decisions you actually make. If it reads like a warning, then be warned and consider changing how you might approach the given situation. If it is hopeful, then pay attention to what it counsels you to do to benefit from the situation even more.

Make Your Own Divination Objects

What you will need:
64 smooth (polished) rocks or 64 cardboard 3 x 3" cards
Paint-pens (found at art stores) to paint on rocks or magic markers to draw on cards
A die for rolling

Paint each hexagram on the rock or card. You can just simply write the number 1 through 64 on each rock or piece of cardboard or draw the lines of the hexagram. You can keep it simple or get as creative as you like.

Consult the I Ching in the same manner recommended on pages 7 and 8 when using your own divination objects. Always hold the cards or rocks while considering your question. Then choose one rock or card for your reading.

If you want to have changing lines to read, which will allow you to obtain a second hexagram, toss the die. Whichever number comes up is the number of changing lines you have. If you roll a 3 then lines 1 through 3 (moving up from the bottom line) are changing lines. You then read those particular line descriptions in the first hexagram, along with reading the main text. To identify a second hexagram, change lines 1 through 3 into their opposite and look up your second hexagram. When reading the second hexagram you will read only the main text and not the individual lines.

After you have consulted the I Ching for a while you may find other ways to design your own divination objects. Traditionally in ancient cultures people either made their own objects or had them handed down from family and community members.

> # Consider
>
> At the end of each hexagram description you'll find additional information that further addresses your concern or question. These sections are intended to give you more guidance and practice in applying the I Ching's counsel.

The Spirit of the I Ching

There are many names for a Higher Power: Spirit, God, the Creator, the Great Unknown, Christ, Buddha, Chi, the Tao, the Mystery, Yahweh, Mother Nature, the Universe, Allah, and the Sage. They are all available to us through the I Ching. Throughout this book, I will refer to Spirit and Higher Power, referring to a spiritual entity that represents a power greater than ourselves, and one that can be contacted through the use of the I Ching. Most often you will find that other books refer to the "Sage" of the I Ching as its spiritual source. You can substitute whatever resonates with your spiritual beliefs.

As you continue to use the I Ching, you will find a deeper, more personal relationship evolving with the Spirit of the I Ching. You will also notice an opening and strengthening within yourself, that you have whatever it takes to live through the changes of life. You will come to realize that the Tao is alive within you. My prayer for you is that you find in here, and in your life, that which you are searching for. That which is beautiful. That which is you.

A Life of Their Own

My dreams are like horses these days; full bodies
running by hot and sweat slicked before I can catch
them, over the crest before I can describe them.
They have a life of their own. I can't be sure they
are my horses; perhaps they've escaped from some
neighboring farm, or are wild, having hidden in the

trees and valleys for a long time before finally
breaking loose across the plains of my sleep.
They elude me, and it is just as well. For I have
lost my rope and halter, and am weaving, wild
myself, and packless, through my own unknown terrain;
no desire to capture, and only the invisible movement,
the muscles of God, leading me on.

—Karen Holden, poet
from Book of Changes: Poems

A Cushion for Your Head

Just sit there right now
Don't do a thing
Just rest.

For your separation from God,
From love,

Is the hardest work
In this
World.

Let me bring you trays of food
And something
That you like to
Drink.

You can use my soft words
As a cushion
For your
Head.

—Hafiz, Sufi master
from The Gift: Poems by Hafiz

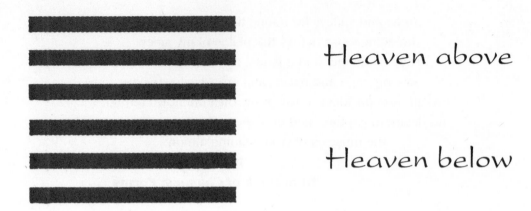

Heaven above

Heaven below

1

Initiation

Most spiritual life calls for times of sudden radical transformation brought about by powerful initiation and rites of passage. For modern young men and women this is a desperate need. If nothing is offered in the way of initiation to prove one's entry into the world of men and women, it will be done unguided in the road or the street, with cars at high speed, with drugs, with weapons.
—Jack Kornfeld, meditation instructor and author of *A Path with Heart*, speaking on Buddhist monastic initiation

The Initiation hexagram represents the ultimate creative force and energy that move everything. The energy that moves the clouds, creates ideas in our minds, and guides the paintbrush across a canvas comes from the same source. This creative energy is active, moving, and always changing. It is the energy behind any initiation. As a teenager you experience many initiations, and perhaps the most significant is the natural rite of passage from adolescence to adulthood.

The creative force is at work in your life right now, and change, in a creative and dynamic way, is occurring. Your creative energy and activity are high. Drawing this hexagram reminds you that you are always creating in your life, and presently you are creating in a positive and dynamic way.

Receiving this hexagram often means that you have come full circle with something, and you are now being rewarded with good feelings about yourself and your life. You may be filled with inspiration, or inspiration may be trying to move through you. At this point in your life your Higher Power is sending you an abundance of help. However, you need to be open and responsive to this energy. This creative power is available to you now, but you can block it by misusing it or ignoring it. If you follow the path of openness and wisdom, profound change will occur.

Be open to your Higher Power by allowing it to guide your actions. In relating to others, practice acceptance and gentleness, because others may not be experiencing the same surge of creativity and help that you are. Share with others in a way that is considerate of their situation and feelings. Your attitude and response to this creative energy will determine your success.

Receiving this hexagram can mean it is time for you to honor this phase of your life by holding some kind of sacred initiation ceremony. Such ceremonies can be simple or complex.

First Line ▬▬

The influence of the creative energy has yet to show up, so it is time to wait. Wait patiently until the time is clearly right. Be careful not to get caught up in negative thinking, doubting that things will work out; they will. Receiving this line may be an indication that it is time to make plans . . . plans for an initiation ceremony or to start some creative project.

Second Line ▬▬

The creative energy is beginning to emerge. When good things enter our lives, it is best to be modest and not go around bragging. Your creativity will be obvious to

Initiation Ceremonies

During the teen years, the quest for the self truly begins. That is why indigenous cultures around the world offer their teens initiation ceremonies such as going on a walkabout in Australia or a vision quest in Native American traditions. An initiation allows you to leave behind your childhood and brings you into the adult world, where you are then recognized and appreciated for your adult qualities. What would represent this to you? What would help you leave behind your childhood and take on the adult life? What could you do to show others that you are mature and capable?

You could have an elaborate ceremony with the help of mentors and adults or a simple ritual. You could also put together a poetry book, run a marathon, or give a performance. It needs to be something that challenges you and proves to yourself and to your community that you are now entering adulthood. Adults in your community need to be involved somehow in this initiation, ideally welcoming you into the adult world. Furthermore, an initiation acknowledges that you are at a vital transition in life, one that affects the entire community. Your initiation, no matter how simple or complex, needs to express your shift from childhood to adulthood.

others. Don't use this increase in creativity and blessings to try to change others' opinions of you. Instead, focus on your creativity. In time, people will gain a better opinion of you based on your behavior.

Third Line ━━━

Great opportunities are yours now, along with much creative energy. Be careful not to sink into doubts, fears, or anxiety. Such feelings often emerge when we are most creative, because we are often taught to doubt ourselves. Try not to be hard on yourself, and let your creative energy flow. Take advantage of this time.

Fourth Line ━━━

You feel confused and pulled in more than one direction. During our young adult years there are many people trying to influence our choices and tell us what to do (and not to do!). Many people, both adults and peers, want to tell you how to use your creative energy. Try not to be overly influenced by their expectations of you, and try to find an answer for yourself. Then, whatever you choose will be right for you.

Fifth Line ━━━━

Others have come to respect you. They value your words and actions. Your peers seek your advice, and adults respect your decisions. You set an example for how the creative intensity of the young adult years can be used.

Sixth Line ━━━━

Sometimes we forget that there are limits to what we can do. During our young adult years we test these limits. This line reminds you that you do have limits to how much you can persuade others. You may see that someone is hurting him- or herself with his or her behaviors, but you can only do so much to positively influence that person. Respect this limit by not pushing yourself on anyone. This may also mean that someone is trying to push him- or herself on you and is therefore having a negative effect on you. The best way to help others is to behave in the way you want them to behave. Focus on your own rite of passage at this time, and others will be positively influenced.

Consider

You might find it helpful to plan an initiation ceremony for yourself or perhaps for yourself and some close friends. You may want to contact a shamanic healer or find an adult who is willing to put some time into creating an initiation ceremony with you. A shamanic healer is one who has been trained to consult the spirit world on our behalf. They can help us retrieve parts of our spiritual selves that have been lost due to trauma and can help us identify our power animals (animals that symbolize our personal power). They are also trained to help people with initiation ceremonies and rites of passage. You can find one in your area by contacting the Foundation for Shamanic Studies at www.shamanism.org. Check out the thunderingyears.com Web site for more links and information about initiation ceremonies.

乾

Also Consider

Where and how do you feel your creativity? What brings you the most happiness when you do it? Are you expressing this creative energy, or are you blocking it somehow? Who will support your creative plans? What creative project might you finish now? If you have never painted, written a poem or letter, or played an instrument, this would be a good time to give it a try.

"The same intelligent, aware force that created and sustains the Universe, which is the Universe, created and sustains us. That intelligent, creative, aware force endlessly shapes and alters us, changes us, to the purpose that we will ultimately come to achieve our true nature and thereafter will keep us forever resonating with the great harmony."

—Wu Wei, I Ching scholar,
from *Wisdom of the I Ching*

Earth above

Earth below

2

Mother Earth

The intelligent person is always open to new ideas.
In fact, he searches for them.
—Proverbs 18:15

There is great skill in learning how to be as receptive as Mother Earth, who can bear so much. This hexagram asks you to be like the earth that receives and nourishes a seed so it can grow into a great tree. One way to be receptive is to practice receiving help from those you trust. Can you be receptive to whatever is happening and learn from the experience? Can you consider advice from others? What is asking for your receptiveness at this time?

This is a good time to be guided by those with good intentions or by our Higher Power. This is a time to be receptive like the earth—to be the one who follows and bears others' counsel. To be receptive means to be open to the Higher Power. Instead of always struggling to make things happen, of fighting against things that are happening, we learn to be more receptive, "go with the flow," and accept the

坤

various ups and downs life has to offer. We are able to do this in part because of our dependence on our Higher Power, much as the seed depends on the earth to nourish it. We don't become extreme and think that life is always good or always bad. And we don't lock others into stereotypes. Instead, we remain more open and receptive to the changes that we all go through as part of our life experience.

Also, this is a time to be receptive to the here and now. Keep your attention on the present situation (it needs your attention), rather than worrying about the future or dwell on the past. We lose our receptiveness, our Mother Earth qualities, when we worry.

First Line ▬ ▬

You are being given some small signs, clues, as to what is to come or what direction you should take. To be receptive to these signs you need to pay attention to what is going on around you and within you. Many signs can appear in your body. What signs is your body giving you about your health? Do you need more rest, better food, less of something? Likewise, there are also signs in relationships. If someone is late for the first date it may be a sign that he or she will likely continue to be late. If he or she is rude to a waitress when eating out, it is a sign of that person's attitude. Instead of minimizing such signs ("oh, it's no big deal"), see them as an indication of what's to come. Make your choices based on these signs.

Receiving this line can also mean being receptive to something you can't change. Perhaps a relationship is at a dead end, or some plan you made isn't going to work out. Some things simply don't work out exactly the way we hoped no matter what we do.

Second Line ▬ ▬

Remain receptive and open. Remember there are many possibilities to every situation. Sit back and wait; you will know what to do in time. Don't react right away; it's better to do less now than to act too quickly.

Third Line ▬ ▬

Being a bit vain is healthy, especially in our young adult years. But too much vanity becomes arrogance and makes it difficult to make wise decisions. When we care too much about how we appear to others, we easily lose sight of what might be best. Don't let the desire to be popular or liked by others (or someone in particular) contradict your Inner Truth. What do you know to be true in this situation? Learn to base your decisions on your beliefs rather than on being accepted by others.

Fourth Line ▬▬ ▬▬

Be careful! Your behavior has brought out negativity in another, either by a mistake you made or because you were misunderstood. You are bothered by this reaction, which is perfectly natural on your part. Try not to retaliate or react. Instead, be receptive to this negativity and leave the person alone. Don't try to prove yourself. Whatever you do, be reserved and cautious. If you are careful and don't get caught up in proving yourself, things will work out.

Fifth Line ▬▬ ▬▬

You are learning to do good without concern about being recognized. This is a sign of great spiritual maturity and a behavior we develop over time—to do good for its own sake. This line also can mean that you are learning to relate to people when they are receptive and open to you, and you pull back when they are closed to you. This too is a great spiritual skill—learning not to give yourself away to someone who is not open to you. It is a waste of time and often has painful results when we become involved in intimate relationships with people who do not truly care about us.

Sixth Line ▬▬ ▬▬

Be careful not to indulge in negative emotions or behaviors such as revenge, doubt, gossip, hate, fear, worry, or being judgmental. Such thoughts and actions will create problems for you. Feeling as if you must act out now will put you in danger because you are caught up in negative emotions. Receiving this line means that you are considering taking a destructive path. If you wait until you feel better and hold more positive thoughts before you act, you will have good results.

坤

Consider

What kind of guidance/answer were you hoping to receive? While using the I Ching, it is important not to focus on your wish for certain answers, because you will miss the wisdom and guidance contained in the reading. Every time you consult the I Ching be open to its guidance. Sometimes you will feel happiness from its guidance, sometimes not, but you should always feel hopeful. Be aware of the type of guidance you want and consider the I Ching's true guidance.

Also Consider

Attitudes such as being judgmental, fearful, hateful, worried, doubtful, and vengeful are learned. So be patient and forgiving of yourself as you unlearn these traits and replace them with compassion, tolerance, hope, faith, love, and optimism. A wonderful book is available to help with this process of unlearning negative habits and creating healthier ones: *The Four Agreements* by don Miguel Ruiz (San Rafael, Calif.: Allen-Amber Publishing, 1997).

"When the pupil is ready,
the teacher will come."
—Eastern saying

Water above

Thunder below

3

Difficulty at First

Most people think of sprouts growing only in spring,
but the ancient Chinese realized that there was a life
force latent in seed form the whole winter . . . The
little plant must overcome the pressure of the soil.
There must be a wholehearted willingness to grow.
—Taoist Master Alfred Huang, from *The Complete I Ching*

Receiving this hexagram is a reminder that, more often than not, there is some difficulty at first when starting something new. Just like the flower that pushes itself through the dark earth, you will get beyond this more challenging time. This can also mean that things are developing "underground." They are not yet seen; nevertheless, growth and change are taking place. You will get beyond this present difficulty if you do not try to force the situation. Take the flower, for example: one does not pull on the stem to make it grow faster. Instead, the natural process of growth and determination push the plant through the soil. Patience and letting nature take

its course are what will work here. Allow the difficulty to move aside on its own, and it will. Ask for help and support from those whom you have trusted over a long period of time. They can help you move through the difficulty.

Most likely, you are feeling restless. This is natural since so much is going on around you, and you sense something good may be happening underneath all the fervent activity. Sometimes we receive this hexagram when we are so stressed and upset with the difficulty that we no longer have a true perspective of the situation. Our thoughts keep us from seeing the latent potential in this situation, often causing us to react in ways that prevent a positive result. This difficulty is temporary and a natural part of something new. A way through the difficulty will emerge. Remember: difficult situations are simply part of the creative life process.

First Line ▬▬▬

This line cautions you to pay attention to the beginning of all relationships and agreements you have with others. The start of any relationship is its foundation, so take it slowly. The beginning always holds some difficulty, so do not force things. If you try to force things you will not see the truth about the other person; you will be too caught up in trying to make certain things happen. This is the time to seek support and advice from your Higher Power and from friends. Is this a good relationship for you to begin?

Second Line ▬▬　▬▬

A solution will come. This is an important time to meditate on your true feelings about a particular person or situation, yourself, and your wishes. What you need to do will be obvious if you take the time to think through the situation first.

Third Line ▬▬　▬▬

This line suggests waiting for the best time to speak your mind or act on your feelings. This is the wisdom of the more advanced spiritual person—to wait for the right moment of opportunity. Do not act impulsively to get through difficulty. If you rush something just because you can't handle the ambiguity of the situation, you prevent the true and good solution from happening. If you push things, you may only make matters worse.

Fourth Line ▬▬ ▬▬

You will find a way to come to an agreement with another person after waiting out the difficulty. When we are confused, it is better to wait until we have obtained some clarity and peace of mind before making a decision.

Fifth Line ▬▬▬

Don't push things beyond the potential of the moment. Don't rush things. Your feelings of anxiety about the difficulty not being completely resolved makes you want to force things to a conclusion. The reality is that life is full of times of ambiguity; becoming skillful at handling these times will make life much better. We can't ever really know how things will turn out. Slow down and trust that you can and will get through this.

Sixth Line ▬▬ ▬▬

Negative emotions such as fear, anxiety, doubt, and hostility cause you to want to ignore what you know to be true. You have reached the "wall" in this situation. Everything has its limits, and you have found the one in this situation. Now is the time to rest and realize that a door will appear through the wall at the right time.

Consider

Can you journal what it is that you are stressed about? Perhaps you can link it to the "new thing" that is coming into your life. Have you started a new relationship or project? Have you moved to a new city? What would help you let go of focusing on the difficult feelings and let things take their course? Journal about your sense of what your next step might be to help you see beyond this initial difficulty. What is the next step you need to take to move this project or relationship along?

An I Ching Journal

Keeping a notebook of your I Ching consultations as well as an account of your thoughts, experiences, and feelings can be a powerful resource for you now and in the future. This journal can be an ongoing reference for you to keep and to check in with. Fill it out with your poetry, drawings, and responses to the "considerations" in this book. You can read over your journal to gain further insight into yourself and your relationship with the I Ching. I have always journaled my consultations, and I have found this to be both a resource and an insight into myself. Karen Holden's book *Book of Changes: Poems* is a result of her journaling poetry during her ten years of consultations with the I Ching (see poem on page 10) Who knows what may come out of your journal!

Never give up.
No matter what is happening,
no matter what is going on around you,
never give up.
—His Holiness the 14th Dalai Lama

Mountain above

Water below

4

Youthful Energy

*Let him who would move the world first
move himself.*
—Seneca proverb

In comparison to the wisdom contained in the I Ching, which is more than two thousand years old, we are new to the spiritual path. This hexagram honors the innocence of our teen years, therefore reminding us of our need to seek wisdom from sources such as the I Ching.

When you receive this hexagram, you're encouraged to seek its counsel and take time to reflect on the message. You can be saved much pain and many mistakes by applying the wisdom embodied in the I Ching (and other ancient sources of wisdom).

The passage into the adult years is a significant one for all on the spiritual path. It is a time of passing from one stage of life into another. It is an intense time for most of us, filled with magic and difficulty. In many ways, we are "in the dark" during this time because we are not certain how things are going to turn out for us. What does my future hold for me? is a question most of us ask during our young adult years. Just as the soil is dark and nurtures the seed, we can accomplish great things in the dark, rich soil of these years.

Much of our potential is still hidden, or at least not fully evolved. It is time now to begin to uncover the wisdom and creativity within ourselves by seeking the help of others who have preceded us on this path. This is the time to commit to a spiritual path, which, generally speaking, means to open up to Spirit in the different forms it takes.

Everyone's life is filled with difficulty and opportunity. By consulting the I Ching wisely and seeking the wisdom of those elders whom you respect, you will travel safely through your teen years. It may be time for you to seek a mentor or spiritual teacher who can offer you further guidance. If you receive this hexagram several times, seek the immediate guidance of a Wisdomkeeper. A Wisdomkeeper is an adult who has traveled the spiritual path with success and can help you on your journey.

This hexagram also speaks to the wisdom within the I Ching itself and how to use its guidance. Use it with a sincere desire to learn and grow and you will benefit from it. Remember to open yourself to the spiritual help that is contained in each reading (review the box "Meditation and the I Ching"). Trust that you are being helped by a Higher Power, and allow this help into your life. Be receptive, as the second hexagram counsels you to do. Try to use each consultation not only to receive advice on what to do, but to gain a larger and deeper perspective of yourself and the world. This is called getting a "cosmic view" of the situation. There is always a bigger picture, a larger perspective to any situation. We just need to take the time to see it.

Sometimes we receive this hexagram when we are too caught up in immature and negative behaviors such as gossiping, ridiculing others, getting even, and being judgmental. Life goes better when we learn to be free of such negative approaches to life's situations. These negative approaches close us down to others and most often make an already difficult situation worse. They also keep us from a more cosmic perspective.

Meditation and the I Ching

Before consulting the I Ching, sit in a meditative posture. Be sure your back is straight but not rigid or too relaxed. Either sit on a cushion on the floor, feet comfortably crossed, or on a chair with your feet on the floor. Sit as still as possible for ten minutes, resting as you breathe. Just simply notice your breath as it moves in and out of the body. Let the breath flow by itself. When you find your mind wandering to thoughts, simply return it gently and kindly to your breath. Notice the physical sensations of your breathing as you sit there, still, awareness on the breath. This allows your mind to settle, making you more receptive to the advice of the I Ching. It also stills the mind, building your inner strength and wisdom.

First Line ▬ ▬

Practice patience and discipline while courageously considering the issue at hand. This means taking a serious look at the situation without beating yourself over the head or analyzing it. Consider your issue while seeking the advice of someone you respect. Listen to those who walk the talk, who set an example. You are learning a new and valuable lesson right now. This lesson can add to your inner strength and wisdom.

Second Line ▬▬▬

It is helpful to learn early in life to be flexible when relating to others. The I Ching counsels us not to hide behind a set way of relating to others (physicians and teachers, sadly, are often expected to relate to their patients and students in a set way; this often creates a chasm in these relationships). Practice seeing everyone's unique qualities. Try not to hold on to a rigid way of relating to others.

Many times throughout our lives we have to deal with the immature behaviors of others, such as someone gossiping or spreading rumors about us. It is best to practice independence and courage by not sinking to their level; don't get caught up in what someone else is saying about you. Learn to see such experiences as an opportunity for you to gain inner strength and independence.

Youthful Energy

Third Line ▬ ▬

It is only human to change one's mind. But be certain that this change of mind is based on inner wisdom and not simply outside circumstances. What looks good on the outside (an attractive person) may not turn out to be so wonderful. Slow yourself down and take a second look at the situation or person that you are inquiring about. This line also counsels us not to be fooled by appearances. A handsome face and charming personality don't always translate to a good heart. Take your time and you will make a wise choice here.

Fourth Line ▬ ▬

Youthful energy can be hazardous when it does not seek the wisdom of someone or some source with more experience. This is the time to seek wise counsel. No one can heal a problem in isolation—reach out for help.

Fifth Line ▬ ▬

When we practice the wisdom contained within the I Ching with a flexible attitude, we will begin to have more understanding about ourselves and our place in the world. Have an open and humble mind, and the mysteries of the universe will be revealed to you.

Sixth Line ▬▬▬

You may be heading down a dead-end road but are too stubborn to admit it. Continuing to be closed off and unwilling to reconsider your choices may lead to more disappointment and difficulty. Try to accept the lesson that comes with this adversity and learn from it. Be gentle with yourself after realizing your mistake.

You may also see another person who is heading down a dead-end path. Witnessing this may bring up negative feelings for you. It can be helpful at such times to remember when you made mistakes and to show some tolerance and compassion for this person. This does not mean that you have to agree with her.

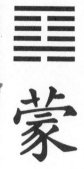

Consider

Try to stop gossiping for an entire week. (Basically, this means not talking about someone who isn't present.) If you can't say something to a person's face, don't say it to anyone. If others are gossiping, either try to change the conversation or walk away. Do your best not to contribute to the gossip by adding to it or by actively listening to it.

After a week of abstaining from gossip, how do you feel? Did you notice how often people tend to gossip? Did you get any insight about why people feel they need to gossip about others? When did you find it difficult (or impossible) not to gossip?

There is a river flowing now very fast,
It is so great and swift that there are those who will be afraid.
They will try to hold on to the shore.
They will feel that they are being torn apart and will suffer greatly.
Know the river has its destination.
The elders say we must let go of the shore, push off
into the middle of the river,
keep our eyes open and our heads above the water.

—A Hopi Elder

Water above

Heaven below

5

Waiting Time

All beings have need of nourishment from above,
but the gift of food comes in its own time, and for
this one must wait.
—Richard Wilhelm and Cary F. Baynes,
from *The I Ching or Book of Changes*, hexagram 5

God is with those who persevere.
—The Qur'an

The I Ching, as well as most spiritual texts, remind us that "perseverance furthers." What does this really mean? It means that most opportunities and breakthroughs come with a lot of faith and patience, as well as effort. Sometimes we get caught up in the effort and forget to include some faith and patience. In receiving this hexagram you are being reminded that this is a time of waiting and patience and that perseverance will further. Your Higher Power will provide a way through when you practice waiting habits such as patience and acceptance. Have you ever rushed something and then have had it not go right because you rushed it? The image of the hexagram is of the clouds in the heavens raining on everything in order to provide nourishment. You too will be nourished.

Life has times when waiting is all we can do. Becoming skillful at waiting can develop our inner strength and happiness. Waiting skillfully means practicing your faith and trusting your Higher Power that things can and do have a way of working out. The I Ching encourages you to engage the power of the Creative by relying more on the wisdom within the I Ching and other sacred texts you've come to appreciate. Engage such ancient wisdom not only by reading the Qur'an or the *Tao-te Ching,* but by practicing their lessons.

It is important at this time not to give in to your doubts and anxiety about the outcome of this concern. The I Ching is telling you that, in part, the purpose of this waiting time is to learn how to wait skillfully. This time can strengthen you. This inner strength is something that is best built up during the young adult years. If you can learn to persevere now, when all seems so urgent and intense, then you will have acquired a powerful skill that will help you throughout your lifetime. This alone will bring you much peace and happiness.

First Line ━━━

Like the hunter or nature enthusiast, you must wait and see what approaches. Getting anxious or thinking too much about the "what ifs" will only cause more stress and difficulty. This line is a strong warning to wait like the hawk for the field mouse, or perhaps to wait like the field mouse until the danger of the hawk is gone. In either case, it is the one who perseveres here who succeeds.

Second Line ━━━

Something or someone may be trying to pull you off balance. Perhaps someone has started a rumor about you. If you keep silent and wait it out, it will pass. You are in a position of strength, and the troublemaker is in a position of weakness. When someone is gossiping or spreading rumors about you, this only speaks to that person's character, not yours. People learn not to trust those who gossip and spread rumors.

Waiting Time

In time, the truth becomes known. The troublemaker will be known for who she or he truly is. There is no need for you to prove yourself at this time.

Third Line ━━━

If you are not careful now, there will be trouble. You are like the field mouse and need to wait out the danger, whatever it may be. It seems as if things are taking forever, but this is just the inner whiner griping about how long it takes for things to work out. Don't listen to this whining voice. Continue to be patient and the outcome will be good. Remember: perseverance furthers!

Fourth Line ━━ ━━

This line warns of great difficulty and maybe even dangerous times. You could be stuck in some kind of troubled relationship or in negative thinking patterns. This is the time to take precautions. You need to free yourself of negative forces by quieting yourself and giving thought to what would be the right thing to do. When you do this, help will come through an insight or person.

Fifth Line ━━━

When life is difficult we are often given a time of rest, a time to collect ourselves. When there is a break in a thunderstorm, which brings some peace and quiet, we too can take advantage of such time to rest and reflect. The difficulty you are involved in is at a resting period but is not over. So, relax and continue to wait, like the hawk that has waited in the tree an entire day for a field mouse to appear.

Sixth Line ━━ ━━

A solution surfaces that at first appears strange; therefore, you may not truly understand it. Keep an open mind and you will see that happiness and solutions come in many shapes and sizes and not always in ways we expect.

Consider

Have you ever watched a hawk wait for its meal of field mouse or rabbit? Spring is a good time to view a hawk perched on a telephone pole or tree waiting for hours, sometimes an entire day, to catch its meal. If the hawk became anxious and began to fly around the field, no mouse or rabbit would come out. Could you sit quietly and watch the hawk wait? Have you ever hunted or sat in the woods waiting for an animal to walk by? It is the perseverance of the hawk, hunter, or nature enthusiast that brings them success. How can you imitate nature and persevere in this situation?

Steady perseverance alone will tame your mind, and it is only
through a tame mind that you can experience God.
—Sathya Sai Baba

Heaven above

Water below

6

Crossroads

To be nobody-but-yourself—in a world which is doing its best, night and day to make you everybody else—means to fight the hardest battle which any human being can fight; and never stop fighting.
—e.e. cummings, poet and painter

In most I Ching translations this hexagram is called Conflict. In Taoist Master Huang's translation it is named Contention and refers to the need to find a way through times of contention and conflict. Here the hexagram is translated into Crossroads as recognition of the valuable and intense stage of life you are presently in: your teen years, or Thundering Years. Your Thunder is all the intensity and energy you experience during your teen years and into your twenties. It is the energy that propels you into your adult years. It is meant to be loud, and even at times scary. How you use and express your Thunder will say a lot about what the rest of your life will be like. This hexagram is asking that you take a look at how you are using this Thunder-energy of yours. For good or harm? What are you doing with your Thunder?

This crossroad, having one foot on the path of childhood and the other on the path of adulthood, causes a constant state of conflict, of Thundering. The I Ching views all conflict as originating within oneself. Receiving this hexagram may mean that you are not handling this time of passage and inner conflict well. It may also mean that you simply need a reminder that the conflict within this passage is a natural one.

Are you accepting the responsibilities and realities of your teen years? How are the conflicts of this crossroad coming up for you? Are you trying to skip this time of transition and take on too many adult responsibilities? Are you in conflict about what choices to make? Are you fighting the transition into adulthood, wanting to remain a child longer? How are you handling the spiritual conflicts that arise at this time in your life? All these are natural conflicts that arise during this time of life.

The I Ching advises us to handle such conflicts with an attitude of flexibility, openness, and acceptance. Be flexible with yourself and others; you are still deciding your life's path and beliefs and dealing with internal conflicts—that's what this crossroad is about. Remain open to all possibilities and to the help of the I Ching. Accept the fact that this stage of life and its conflicts are a necessary part of a person's spiritual development. It can't be avoided entirely.

This crossroad into adulthood is filled with possibilities, obstacles, decisions, challenges, intense but short-term relationships, and, ultimately, finding yourself and your place in the world. How could such a journey be free of conflict?

First Line ━━ ━

At this time in your life, it is very important to do what you know is correct. This is because decisions that you make now are the foundation for the rest of your life. This is the wisdom taught within the I Ching—for us to make decisions that are correct and just. We are counseled to make choices that resonate with an inner sense of truth and to not react quickly to conflict. Take your time to discover the best decision for you. When we respond to conflict this way, the results are good.

Crossroads

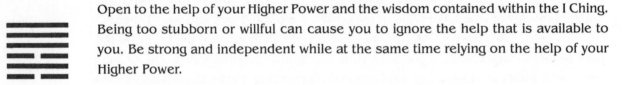

Second Line ━━━━

Open to the help of your Higher Power and the wisdom contained within the I Ching. Being too stubborn or willful can cause you to ignore the help that is available to you. Be strong and independent while at the same time relying on the help of your Higher Power.

Third Line ━━ ━━

The conflict of this time may be intense for you right now. How might you apply the wisdom of others who have gone before you and succeeded with similar conflicts? What traits of theirs might you imitate at this time? Many wise people have success-fully made it through the crossroads of youth. How did they do it?

Fourth Line ━━━━

Focus on the present situation. Focus on *what* needs your attention now. Beware of being worried about the future. Although it is important to dream and plan at this time of your life, most of your attention needs to be on the present. Receiving this line may be a call for you to bring yourself more into the present.

Fifth Line ━━━━

You are in a conflict that needs to be given over to your Higher Power. Tell yourself to "let go and let God," or ask yourself "What would the Buddha do?" Trust that good can come out of this conflict when you don't get yourself caught up in it. When you let it go, great happiness can result.

Sixth Line ━━━━

You tend to get wrapped up in worrying or keep an argument going when it is best to move on to the next issue at hand. Practice letting go and notice the good that unfolds.

Consider

There were four teens journeying on the path of life when they came across a huge rock in the middle of the path. Next to it was a beautiful vase that had been shattered. It was obvious that at one time this vase was worth a great deal of money and sentimental value. All four stopped and looked down at the rock and broken vase.

The first young adult asked, "Why? Why would God let such a thing happen? Perhaps it is proof that there is no God after all." This person began to think about all the horrors and pain that existed in the world and "why, why, why would God let this be, if God truly loved us?" This person slumped down next to the path in a state of depression and hopelessness.

The second young adult asked, "How? How did this happen? Who is to blame here? Did the rock hit the vase or the vase hit the rock?" This person thought about who was causing all the trouble in his life qnd who was to blame for all the pain in the world. Someone, he thought, is responsible for all this suffering and pain. And if we can just figure out how this suffering happens—who is the cause, then we can get rid of them!" This young person circled around and around the vase and the rock in an increasing state of anxiety.

The third young adult, it is told, had been smoking pot and blindly stumbled upon the broken vase, cut herself, and walked off into the woods in denial. She is still lost in the woods.

The fourth young person bent over the vase and the rock and laughed a bit. He said, "I don't know why such a thing happens. It is a question we all have. I too wonder why God lets such things happen, but this I cannot answer today. It is a mystery to me. And, I cannot answer how this happens. I was not here to witness whether the rock hit the vase or the vase hit the rock. All I know is *what* happened. All I know is the jar is broken." This young person carefully bent down and picked up the broken shards of glass and placed them in a large pocket in his jacket and continued to walk the path of life. As he walked, the sounds of the shards in his pocket sounded a bit like wind chimes.

Can you approach the present conflicts with the question of what is happening and what you want to do about it? Can you let the question of "Why" be part of the mystery we all share and remain open to this question instead of getting stuck in fear and anxiety? Can you let go of having to blame someone (including yourself) for any pain that is in your life right now? Instead, can you focus on what needs to be done to move forward on your path of life?

Earth above

Water below

7
Spiritual Warriors

Life shrinks or expands in proportion to one's courage.
—Anaïs Nin, author of *Under a Glass Bell*

A man with outward courage dares to die
A man with inward courage dares to live.
—Lao-tzu, ancient Taoist sage and author of *Tao-te Ching*

The I Ching recognizes that at this time of our lives we begin the journey of a Spiritual Warrior. We are "warriors" because many challenges, or "battles," will be part of our journey into adulthood. The battles of the Spiritual Warrior are ones of the heart and mind. Receiving this hexagram means that you are at battle with some spiritual issue that you need to conquer or understand. This is an opportunity

to learn a new skill and to gather wisdom you will need throughout your entire life.

You are advised to prepare for a "test" or battle. You are counseled to use such skills as listening to your inner wisdom, seeking counsel, persevering, being alert, acknowledging your inner independence, and being just to win the battle. You will discover that the use of these spiritual skills can bring success as well as the help of others when you need it.

First Line ▬▬ ▬▬

Justness is called for here. Is your response to the situation just? Use this time to develop the skill of being just. This can improve the situation at hand. Being just means being fair and considerate to all concerned, including yourself.

Second Line ▬▬▬▬

Seeking the counsel of others is called for here. Are you seeking counsel from a mentor, spiritual advisor, or a Higher Power? Every step of the path requires the help of our Higher Power. You will find this help when you ask for it with sincerity and patience.

Third Line ▬▬ ▬▬

Perseverance and patience are called for here. Are you being patient with yourself? Sometimes we are toughest on ourselves. A great Warrior knows how to wait and when to act.

Fourth Line ▬▬ ▬▬

Inner independence is called for here. Even though others act badly, do not sink to their level. Disengage and be strong. Being inwardly independent means to believe in oneself and not to be swayed by negative circumstances.

Fifth Line ▬▬ ▬▬

Inner wisdom is called for here. Focus on such inner principles as letting go of grievances even though others have done wrong. Inner wisdom means trusting the truth that lies within you, especially during difficult times.

Spiritual Warriors

Sixth Line ▬▬ ▬▬

Alertness is called for here. The battle has been won, or is about to be won. For the Spiritual Warrior this is often the time when alertness is most important because it is when we tend to be too self-satisfied and forget where our help came from. Enjoy the success while at the same time holding on to spiritual integrity. Remain alert.

Consider

There are many books available on Spiritual Warriorship. Here are a few I recommend:

The Fourfold Way: Walking the Paths of the Warrior, Teacher, Healer, and Visionary by Angeles Arrien, Ph.D. (San Francisco: HarperSanFrancisco, 1993).

Rainbow Tribe: Ordinary People Journeying on the Red Road by Ed McGaa (San Francisco: HarperSanFrancisco, 1992).

Return of the Bird Tribes by Ken Carey (Kansas City: A UniSun Book, 1988).

The Teachings of Don Juan and Journey to Ixtlan: The Lessons of Don Juan by Carlos Castaneda (New York: Simon and Schuster, 1968 and 1972).

The Thundering Years: Rituals and Sacred Wisdom for Teens by Julie Tallard Johnson (Rochester, Vt.: Bindu Books, 2001).

Water above

Earth below

8

The Sacred Dance of Love

Sing and dance together and be joyous, but let each one of you be alone, even as the strings of a lute are alone though they quiver with the same music.

—Kahlil Gibran, Lebanese poet, philosopher, and author of *The Prophet*

This hexagram is about intimate relationships and how to have and maintain a close and loving union with another person. When you receive this hexagram you are encouraged to seek loving relationships with others—not isolation. We all need to be close to those who care about us. Sometimes we use isolation to deal with our problems. Isolation is when we avoid others, become truant, hide out watching too

much television, and in general avoid the challenges of intimate relationships. You are recommended to make a genuine connection with other people.

When making a connection with others it is important not to become overly possessive or willing to be possessed by another. Let each one of you be an individual. The sacred dance of love is about being in a close relationship with others while at the same time being able to be alone. The image that goes with this hexagram is of water over earth. Imagine the relationship between the river and the earth. The river feeds the earth; the earth holds the water. They are intimately connected, but they are also separate—the river contains an entire life of its own. Can you create this kind of togetherness with others? Can you be strong alone while at times being close and intimate with someone? Can you let others go their own way when they need to while being there to support them in times of need? This is a sign of a true and mature love, one that is not possessive or overly dependent.

The I Ching also recommends that you let the love of your Higher Power into all your relationships. We do this by remembering that the ultimate dance of love is also with the Creator, as we understand him or her.

First Line — —

It is important to have honesty as the foundation of any relationship. First be truthful with yourself and then with the one you are seeking closeness with. Are you being honest with yourself about this person? Is honesty the foundation of the relationship you are inquiring about?

Second Line — —

Trust your heart and inner wisdom. Seek others who support and strengthen you, who respect your truth and principles. When we seek others with an open heart and inner wisdom, positive relationships result.

Third Line — —

Be careful not to throw yourself into a wrong relationship. Take the time needed to get to truly know a person before committing to anything. In receiving this line, it's possible that you are considering compromising your truth and principles just to be accepted by someone else (or a group of others). Nothing good can come of compromising yourself in such a way. A positive and loving relationship would never require that you give up your principles.

Fourth Line — — — —

Stay strong and true to your beliefs and good will come to you in the form of loving and healthy relationships. Receiving this line is a reminder, however, that there is more to life than finding the right boyfriend or girlfriend. Don't lose sight of all that is of value to you while searching for that one relationship. A true and loving relationship will be the result of your living a life full of many interests and people.

Fifth Line ————

Trying to force a relationship will never work. A true and lasting love relationship happens somewhat naturally: you find each other while being involved in activities you enjoy. Remember, too, that our young adult years are typically a time to have many relationships, as we are discovering who we are and who we want to spend our lives with.

Sixth Line — — — —

Trust is not something we give away to others early on; it is a gift. Our trust is something others need to earn. Have those you are inquiring about earned your trust?

Consider

"There are fifty ways to leave your lover," as the old Paul Simon tune reminds us. How many ways can you come up with to end a relationship in a respectful and compassionate way? Make a list of these in your journal, or write your own verse about fifty (or ten) ways to leave your lover.

Most of us find it very difficult to end relationships, even those that are bad or dangerous for us. But in fact, we all have to end many relationships during our lifetime, such as leaving a group, a friend, a club, or a lover. Many people are afraid to get into relationships because they don't know how to get out of one if they need to. You can refer back to the ideas in your list when the time comes to end a relationship.

Wind above

Heaven below

9

Starting Small

Make a small thing great, and the few into many.
Take on the largest things when they're still small,
Start the hardest things while they're still easy.
—Lao-tzu, ancient Taoist sage and author of *Tao-te Ching*, 33 (Element)

If left to its natural wisdom, the most polluted lake or river will return to a healthy condition. However, if the water is badly polluted, it will take nature many, many, many small steps to return the water to a healthy state. Nothing is ever beyond repair, if it can be left to its own potential. This is true for you and the situation about which you inquire. Through small steps much can and will be gained.

This is the time to build up strength, to prepare for the next step, to acquire wisdom about the situation; this is not the time to act grandiose. Don't leap from tall buildings like a superhero; rather, build up and restore your strength so your natural potential can come forth at the right time. It is like the building up of rain clouds for a great downpour. The image is one of wind blowing across the sky and pushing the clouds around. But rain is not expected yet. The time now is to build up your inner qualities such as wisdom, compassion, intuition, and strength. Once you have these stored up, step by step, there will come a time to use them.

Receiving this hexagram can mean that something is pressuring you to take a grandiose step when small steps are best. What small action can be taken to move you toward your desired goal?

Outside circumstances are likely limiting you (the water is already polluted), so taking small steps to help the situation reach its natural potential will have positive results. How might you do this? How can you gather strength and wisdom in this situation? You may also need to gather some support from friends and family. A lake does not return to a healthy state from a polluted state on its own: it naturally gathers the support and help of every living creature and plant in its ecosystem. A small step for you may be asking for help from those who can help you. This is how small becomes powerful—through its gathering of wisdom, strength, and support, step by step.

First Line ━━━━

This can be a very favorable time. Remain content with taking small steps and building up your strength and wisdom. Do not try to force a change for the better. Trust that your Higher Power is acting on your behalf. You might say that the polluted lake's Higher Power is Nature, which helps the lake restore itself to its natural, beautiful state. You too have this Power available to you.

Second Line ━━━━

Receiving this line may mean that you need to seek the support of someone you already trust. It is not the time to act; it is the time to get the support of another like-minded friend or mentor. The small step of obtaining the support of a friend or mentor can bring on positive results. This also is the time to build up your intuitive abilities by reflecting on the times that you trusted your "gut" and the times you did not.

Third Line ———

Your wanting to rush things will only bring on disappointment. Perhaps you have your mind set on someone who is not right for you. Usually we want to push things when our intuition tells us it is not the right time or person. We do this because our desires override our intuition and inner wisdom. Trying to force things makes us blind to the truth. Try to slow down and listen to your inner wisdom.

Fourth Line —— ——

Continue to build up your inner strength and wisdom and good fortune will surround you.

Fifth Line ———

When we succeed at building up our inner wisdom and inner strength, we then find these qualities in others. Our goodness brings out the goodness in others. You are able to help others because you have helped yourself. You will experience great happiness as a result of sharing your happiness with others.

Sixth Line ———

It is time to rest now, because you have gathered to yourself many good qualities and with them good fortune. Just as the rain cloud releases its rain, you have released the potential of this situation. If we continue collecting without rest we will only wear ourselves down.

Consider

Pay attention to what you tend to collect in your life. Are you a collector of some kind? Do you collect rocks, dolls, art, poetry, spiritual symbols? How might these physical collectibles represent who you are as a person? How might they be symbolic of inner qualities you are collecting? Some people collect stories, some Beanie Babies, while others collect football paraphernalia. How long did it take you to acquire your collec-

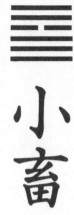

tion thus far? Isn't it true that collections are in part precious because they are collected, piece by piece, over time?

Now consider what thoughts, beliefs, and characteristics you are collecting and therefore building upon. Do you find you collect a lot of negative beliefs and stories? Do you read and listen to a lot of negative drama? Or, do you collect more life-enhancing stories, such as the underdog stories in which the weaker or troubled person comes through to succeed somehow. What ideas do you collect? We all tend to find ideas and "evidence" that back up our own beliefs. What might these be for you? Could you practice collecting a certain kind of story and idea and see where that leads you?

Collect compassion and bring it into your life for ten days. Collect stories, ideas, and experiences that are compassionate. Include experimenting with being compassionate to at least one person a day. Try to collect one story about compassion each day, or find a poem that elicits feelings of compassion inside you. What do you think will be the result of collecting compassion for ten days?

The wind restrains the clouds, the rising breath of the Creative,
and makes them grow dense, but as yet is not strong enough
to turn them to rain.
**—Richard Wilhelm and Cary F. Baynes,
from *The I Ching or Book of Changes*, hexagram 9**

Heaven above

Lake below

10

Caution

People are always blaming their circumstances for what they are. I don't believe in circumstances. The people who get on in this world are the people who get up and look for the circumstances they want, and, if they can't find them, make them.
—George Bernard Shaw, playwright

An image associated with this hexagram is that of someone walking on a tiger's tail without being bitten. Can you imagine the skill it would take to walk on a tiger's tail without bringing any harm to yourself? Yet, we all find ourselves in very difficult and sensitive situations. You are likely in one at this time. To walk through danger or difficulty, or to even bear a very uncomfortable situation, takes discipline and personal responsibility. Studies of successful and happy individuals show that such people do not blame their difficulties on others and take responsibility for their situations. It is not a quality of a spiritually mature person to blame others for his or her circumstances. Instead, this uncomfortable or difficult situation is understood as an opportunity to practice principles such as discipline and courage.

If we get too cocky, the tiger will surely consume us. If we get too angry or even scared, the tiger will consume us. How can you be careful enough in this situation so as not to get into more serious trouble and difficulty? Being careful includes being respectful to others, especially those less fortunate than ourself. This hexagram calls on us to develop social skills that will help us in difficult situations. For example, you are waiting in a long line, but when you get to the front, the tickets are sold out. Do you take it out on the counter help? What attitudes are building up inside as you wait for your ticket? Perhaps the person selling tickets has two tickets hidden in her back pocket. Kindness and respect bring rewards.

First Line ━━━

When you begin to feel better and are getting out of the difficult situation, be sure to remain cautious. You are still on the tail of the tiger! When we get too cocky about our successes, we tend to overstep our bounds and get hurt.

Second Line ━━━

There is happiness in knowing what it is we need to do and doing it. Regardless of what others might think of you, you choose to do what you know to be correct, and this helps to resolve the difficulty.

Third Line ━━ ━━

We get "bitten" when we get too pushy. When we try to push ourselves on others, they usually push back. To force yourself or your wishes on others is not being careful and can result in more difficulty for you and others.

Fourth Line ━━━

Practicing skills such as caution and thoughtfulness while you are treading through difficulty brings you success and happiness. Thoughtfulness includes reflecting on what it is you did to help create this difficulty as well as how to best get out of it without harming yourself or others.

Fifth Line ━━━

You are learning to unite strength with caution. This can bring continued success and carry you through the present difficulty. Also, the I Ching encourages you to further cultivate these skills in order to develop yourself and benefit others.

Sixth Line ━━━

Such personal qualities as inner strength, caution, and acceptance move mountains and give you what it takes to tread safely on the tail of a tiger. Remember: brute force and pushing yourself on others will only result in additional problems.

Receiving this line can mean that it is a good time to consider your experience with this present difficulty. How did it start? How have you related to the difficulty thus far? What have you done to make it worse or better? What can you learn from reviewing the situation carefully? Doing such a review can help prepare you for future difficulties or may even help prevent them.

Consider

The Tiger and the Fox

Once there was a young woman who longed to know her place in the world and how to listen to God's wisdom. She went for a walk through the woods and saw a fox that had lost its legs, and she wondered how it lived. She waited and watched. At dusk she saw a great tiger with some wild game in its mouth. He had eaten much of it but took the rest of the meat to the fox. And the fox happily ate it.

The next day the young woman watched again and saw the tiger once again bring some fresh game to the fox to eat. The young woman was moved by how God provided for the fox by means of the tiger. She thought, "That must be it! I am meant to go sit quietly in the woods and God will provide for me all that I need as well!" So, the next day she went out to a deep spot in the woods where she sat herself up against a tree and waited. She waited for God to bring her what she needed and believed God would take care of her in the same way the fox was taken care of. Many days and nights passed, and the young woman was on the verge of starvation and death. As she lay her head down in defeat she heard a voice shouting at her: "Wake up, foolish girl, open your eyes to the truth! Follow the example of the tiger and stop imitating the disabled fox!"

Earth above

Heaven below

11

Peace of Mind

My feeling is, the better we feel about ourselves,
the fewer times we have to knock somebody down
in order to stand on top of their bodies and feel tall.
—Odette Pollar, author of *Dynamics of Diversity*

In this hectic world and this challenging time of the teen years, having peace of mind can be a great feat. By applying the principles suggested throughout the I Ching, we are guaranteed to accomplish a feeling of inner peace.

So what does "peace of mind" really mean? It means that we are not caught up in negative thoughts, such as worrying, judging ourselves or others harshly, or ruminating about the past. When we have peace of mind we are not comparing ourselves to others, which always makes us feel estranged from the one(s) we are comparing ourselves to. Either they come across as better, so we don't approach them, or not as good as we are, so we distance ourselves from them. To have peace of mind means

that we are at peace with ourselves, that we are good company for ourselves.

This hexagram also reflects outer circumstances, which have an uncanny way of matching our inner circumstances. As you can see, this hexagram is balanced—heaven and earth are in balance. The image is "heaven on earth," with heaven (below) placing itself below earth (above). Being in balance brings us peace of mind. One way to have peace of mind is to bring your outer world of relationships, projects, and plans into balance (alignment) with the inner world of thoughts, feelings, and attitudes. For example, when we feel good about ourselves, these positive feelings are reflected in our good relations with others. The I Ching counsels us that it is the outer world that comes into balance with the inner world, not the other way around. So, working on our inner selves brings us more happiness in the outer world of relationships.

Receiving this hexagram also means that you have either attained some peace in your life or are about to. If you have just come out of a difficult time, know that peace is at hand. This peace is due to your effort to work on yourself—so now the outer world is coming into alignment with these positive efforts.

First Line ━━━

This is a good time for you to begin a project or to start a new job. To succeed with your endeavor, reach out for the support of your friends, peers, and coworkers. Search for others who have similar ideals and goals.

Second Line ━━━

As you begin a new project, always be cautious and aware of what you are getting yourself into. Pay attention to what you are committing to and what you hope to get in return. This kind of attentiveness can bring good results for you and others involved in the project. Also, be sure that you are ready and willing to finish what you have started.

Third Line ━━━

The universal principle "nothing is permanent; everything is always in flux," or "everything changes; nothing remains the same," is true of times of peace and balance as well. When things change and become difficult again do not get discouraged or be hard on yourself. Don't try to hold on to the peaceful times. Instead, accept the changes and remember the inner strength you have acquired. Peaceful times will return if you remain true to yourself.

Fourth Line ▬▬ ▬▬

Sometimes we want to impress others with our successes, but there should be balance to this as well. We need to show off without putting ourselves above others. We need to be sensitive to the situations of others while we are experiencing success: they may be having a down time. Happiness is assured when you share your success in a modest and balanced way.

Fifth Line ▬▬ ▬▬

Receiving this line means that you have solicited the help of your Higher Power. You are in a state of grace and benefit. So relax and be patient; things are working out to your benefit. With regard to others, continue to be modest and sincere with them, and align yourself with good people.

Sixth Line ▬▬ ▬▬

This time of peace and success has reached its peak, and must decline as all things in nature do. In reality there are limits to how high we can go, or how far we can reach. You have reached a limit. Accept this and be patient: there is always a return to peace and success.

Consider

To help obtain peace of mind when you are caught up in negative thinking, try this exercise. Describe your negative thought in your journal. Then, write an opposite, more positive affirmation. For example: Negative thought—"Everyone at work thinks all I care about is myself and that I am arrogant." Affirmative thought—"I care about others' feelings and want to get along with others." Then date the journal. When you find yourself caught up in such negative thinking, practice letting it go. Instead of building on it like a story, stop thinking about it. Repeating the affirmative thought will help you focus on something else. Then, after repeating the positive thought, put your focus on something else, preferably whatever it is you are doing at the time. If you are working, put your full attention on that; if you are eating, enjoy every bite; and, if you are washing the dishes, put your thoughts on washing the dishes. Practice this enough and you will acquire peace of mind.

Heaven above

Earth below

12

Boredom

Be patient toward all that is unresolved in your heart and try to love the questions themselves.
—Rainer Maria Rilke, German poet

When people are bored, it is primarily with their own selves that they are bored.
—Eric Hoffer, author, from *Zen Soup*

Boredom can be a most challenging state of mind. And it is a state of mind, due not entirely to outside circumstances. For some reason we are experiencing a time of boredom, where nothing really seems to be happening. Or, we may be relating to others in a bored way, uninterested in their lives and circumstances. The most we can do to break this boredom is work on our own attitude.

Times of boredom are quite common during our teen and young adult years. One reason is that we don't have as much control and authority in our lives as we would like. We sometimes feel stuck in our classes, stuck in relationships, stuck at home, stuck in a job we don't really like. This stuckness gets translated into boredom. Then, to bust out of this boredom, we may do things that cause us harm; we act out of balance. We abuse drugs and alcohol, drive too fast, binge on junk food, take dangerous risks, have unsafe sex, get angry with strangers, destroy property that doesn't belong to us . . . These may be extremes, but they are not all that uncommon. Other times we sink deeper into our boredom by spending too much time in front of the television or playing video games; or, we get further stuck in a relationship that feels like a dead end.

To avoid getting to a place where you have to bust your way out of boredom, or sink further into it, work with the boredom. The truth is there will always be times in life when you feel bored—when you feel stuck. So the I Ching is counseling us that this time of boredom is inevitable. It is what we do with it that is going to make a difference, because avoiding it is not possible.

Receiving this hexagram acknowledges that you are in a state of boredom. Now, while you are feeling bored, is a good time to ask yourself: "What is it I would like to be doing now?" Can you turn this boredom into creative energy by working on or starting something creative? While bored, it is a good time to consider what you want to be doing with your life—what would get you excited and motivated? Need to apply for a new job? Want to learn how to fly a helicopter or travel to a new place? Have you always wanted to begin that special project? Now would be a good time to put some thought into making your wishes real. Now is also a good time to practice the principles offered throughout the I Ching. Focus your mind on what principles you want to develop, and you can move out of the boredom.

First Line ━━ ━━

You are feeling overwhelmed and agitated by your state of boredom. Do your best to get through it. Find ways to uplift yourself, such as through journaling, meditating, exercising, writing poetry, visiting with friends, or attending a concert or seminar that will uplift you.

Second Line ▬ ▬

Practice tolerance and patience in dealing with that which is boring and stuck in your life at this time. Make every effort to not bring the boredom to an end through violent or harmful means. By persevering and practicing tolerance, you benefit yourself and those around you.

Third Line ▬ ▬

Those who have tried to influence you in a negative way can get in trouble because of it. Sometimes others deal with their boredom by trying to engage us in wrong action. Be understanding but try not to get involved. Others who witness your strength may join you. This can bring an end to your boredom.

Fourth Line ▬▬▬

Only when we succeed at following the Higher Path with the help of our Higher Power do we find that others seek our company. Focus on developing good qualities and the situation can improve.

Fifth Line ▬▬▬

Change is at hand. Don't give up, and be patient. Boredom can be transformed easily into a dynamic time when we hang on to good intentions.

Sixth Line ▬▬▬

The boredom can end when you use your inner strength. Allow your inner wisdom and the wisdom of your Higher Power to transform the boredom. Happiness and good energy are the results.

Consider

Take some time to name more specifically what it is that feels so boring to you. Everything? A relationship? A class? This time of life? This time of year? Now, using your imagination, ask yourself what you would prefer to be doing right now. Without holding back, make a list of activities or accomplishments you want to experience. Don't leave any out; include the ones that may even be considered harmful or bad. Write this list out without stopping. Then, go over the list and cross out any of those that could cause you or others harm in any way. Circle in red those that seem the most realistic to you right now. These are the ones you feel you could achieve or start soon. Then circle in blue the ones that really get you psyched when you think of doing them (realistic or not). Make a separate list that includes those you circled with both red and blue.

Now, choose something from your final list and start making it happen. Even if it is unrealistic at this time, isn't there something you can do to make a move toward it? Let's say one idea you have is to attend a concert in a nearby city. But you don't have enough money and haven't decided who you want to go with. And, you have yet to go into the city without your parents. There is a lot you could do to start making your attendance at the concert a reality. Earn some money and talk to friends or family about going. Call a friend right now who might have an idea about how to get there.

No matter how difficult the situation, to the Chinese there is always a point where it turns favorable. In this way, hope always lies ahead.
—Taoist Master Alfred Huang,
from *The Complete I Ching,* hexagram 12

Heaven above

Fire below

13

Lovers, Friends, and Like-minded People

I feel the capacity to care is the thing which gives life its deepest significance and meaning.
—Pablo Casals, Spanish musician

This hexagram refers to the best and most favorable foundation for relationships. You need to take a look at the foundations of your present relationships. And if you are inquiring about a particular relationship, ask yourself what it is that you and the other person are bringing into this relationship. All healthy relationships are founded on respect, honesty, mutual regard, and kindness and share common principles such as those expressed throughout the I Ching. Receiving this hexagram means that you need to evaluate your present relationships.

Incredible things can take place when like-minded people come together. When we have shared principles and interests we have more energy and creativity to follow through with our plans. Great things can be accomplished when two or more people come together for loving and respectful reasons. When two or more people come together for negative reasons, these relationships affect us adversely. They typically drain us of the vital and creative energy we need to live a fulfilling life.

One important element in a caring relationship is trust. But trust should not be given away easily. It is something others need to earn. We can go into a relationship open to its many possibilities and offer our trust only when the other person has proven him- or herself trustworthy. Just because we want to trust the other person doesn't make him or her trustworthy. To trust others blindly usually results in disappointment. This is the time to take a look at your relationships so that you can develop strong, loving bonds with others.

First Line ━━━

Injurious secrets and dishonesty cause trouble and pain in our relationships. Are you being asked to keep a secret that feels wrong? Bring honesty into your relationships and hold on to what you know to be good and true. This inner strength can bring positive results.

Second Line ━━ ━━

Forming a group or gang in which you intentionally bash or exclude others will inevitably result in misfortune. Are you considering joining a group that puts themselves above others? When relationships are built on hate, exclusion, or arrogance the outcome is ill fated. If you send out hate, negativity, and arrogance that is inevitably what you will get back. Furthermore, such relationships consume a lot of energy, taking away from other important things in life.

Third Line ━━━

Not being open to others and keeping injurious secrets are leading to more distrust and secrets. No good can come from this. Try to step back and seek guidance from your Higher Power. Are these relationships offering you what you want? It is okay to walk away from harmful relationships.

Fourth Line ━━

Misunderstanding and the arguments that result from miscommunications separate people. Do what you can to understand the other person's point of view. This doesn't mean that you agree with that person, but you can come to an understanding and acceptance of a different point of view. This can give you a great and positive influence on the other person and harmony can result. Sometimes harmony comes through letting the other person go his or her own way.

Fifth Line ━━

There will be a reunion with someone you are separated from, but not yet. Unity is inevitable. Be patient, don't push yourself on them, and remain open to this person in your heart.

Sixth Line ━━

Now you gain an understanding that the spiritual path with ideals such as compassion, openness, and patience is the only true path. However, you hold some doubt and reservation about this realization, and this causes you to feel confused. Remember: many doors can open as you bring such wisdom and love into all your relationships.

Consider

Intentions are powerful. They are the very first building blocks of any relationship or endeavor. Intentions are what we each bring into an experience—they define what we want to get out of it. Everything that follows in a relationship depends on our intentions and the intentions of the other person. What are your intentions in your various relationships? Can you identify what the other person's intentions are? For example, if you feel used or ignored in a relationship, it is likely that these feelings match the other person's intentions.

What are you expecting in this relationship? Are you being honest with yourself and with this person about what it is you want and hope for? The clearer you can be about your intentions, the better the results.

Fire above

Heaven below

14

Inheritance

Deciding to focus on our freedom isn't selfish; it is the greatest gift we can give to humanity.
—don Miguel Ruiz, author of
The Four Agreements Companion Book

The image of this hexagram is that of the sun shining high in the sky and offering light and energy to everything below. This is a time of great power and potential. You are receiving an "inheritance" from "Heaven," from your spiritual source. It is a time of harvest and abundance for you. It is time to use your inheritance wisely.

During your teen years, on into your young adult years, you are likely to receive this hexagram often. This is a time in your life when you are "inheriting" your own power—you likely feel this with intense surges of emotion and physical excitement. If you learn to claim and use this power in a creative and respectful way, it can offer you strength and more inheritances throughout your lifetime. Be conscientious in

practicing the principles outlined throughout the I Ching. Balance these times of intensity and power with reflection and rest, and the inheritances will last.

This is also a time for you to gain more understanding about yourself, the world around you, and your place in the circle of life. These understandings are also inheritances from your spiritual source and are given to you because you are ready to receive them, because you have been applying the principles offered to you by the I Ching. For example, you have come to understand that small things matter (hexagram 9).

How you start something has a great affect on how it progresses. When you overlooked this small step, you likely created more difficulty for yourself. So, now you understand that small steps count, and you pay more attention to what is happening in the moment. This understanding is transformed into the way you relate to your life, and thus you have "inherited" spiritual knowledge.

Inheritance can also come in the form of an improvement in a situation, or an inheritance of money, or a reunion with someone with whom you have been estranged. With all your inheritances, remain humble. Being humble means that you remain grounded in the truth that you did not get this inheritance all on your own—your spiritual source brought it to you. Remaining humble allows each of us to inherit more because we remain accessible to Spirit and its help.

First Line ━━━━

During such intense times of power and inheritance it is important that you don't get thrown off balance. Your peace of mind is often challenged when you experience a time of great abundance. Practice humility and show gratitude to your spiritual source, and your inheritance will endure.

Second Line ━━━━

The greatest inheritance you can possess is the qualities of inner peace, inner strength, and equanimity. Equanimity is often expressed through a nonjudgmental attitude. With these internal possessions, you can get through all the ups and downs of life.

Third Line ━━━

This line suggests that you share your inheritance with others who appreciate qualities such as those mentioned in line two. To give yourself or your inheritances away to those who do not appreciate you is foolish. Be generous with your possessions and thoughtful at the same time.

Fourth Line ━━━

Comparing yourself to others will always result in unhappiness and loneliness. Are you making yourself out to be better than others? Or, are you making others out to be better than you? This only puts a wedge between you and them, making happy relationships impossible. It is okay to not like someone. But can you do this in a way that allows them to go their way and you to go yours?

Fifth Line ━━ ━━

Even though you have come into a great inheritance, do not give it all away. There is such a thing as being too giving. This means that you actually give more than you realistically have to offer. Let's say you just inherited a positive attitude. Giving this all away to others would be like always pretending to be happy and positive, when this just isn't possible. Or, it is like giving love to someone who doesn't love you, so you are left feeling used. Be aware of how you share yourself and your inheritances with others.

Sixth Line ━━━

The greatest blessings and inheritances are given to those who are true to their spiritual path and are considerate of others.

大有

Consider

Make an altar that symbolizes your connection to, reliance on, and appreciation of your spiritual source. An altar can be a small table, a cloth on the floor, or a section of a shelf. Some people put their altars outside or in a window.

An altar is a place for you to place items that express your spiritual truths and symbolize your inheritances. It is a place to acknowledge and communicate with the Higher Power. It can include incense, candles, pictures (of spiritual figures or people that you love), religious symbols, power objects, your I Ching coins or sticks, or any object that reminds you of what's important to you. Many people have photographs or figurines of Wisdomkeepers such as the Buddha or Jesus Christ on their altars. Place your prayers or questions on the altar, along with inspiring poems or quotes.

The altar can be a place for you to meditate and pray, using it as a focal point. It can be a place where you visit your Higher Power and consult the I Ching.

All that we behold is full of blessings.
—William Wordsworth, English poet

Earth above

Mountain below

15

Being Grounded

Your own mind is a sacred enclosure into which nothing harmful can enter except by your permission.
—Arnold Bennett, journalist, novelist

"Being grounded" is about not being extreme in our thoughts or actions. Perhaps you have heard someone say, "She is grounded in reality." In the I Ching we are taught that we have limits and boundaries but no rules. No rules! The I Ching does not push rules on us. Rather, it is a guide for us, showing us the many possibilities life has to offer. It also guides us toward an understanding of ourselves and our world, which includes the limits placed on us by nature. Limits and boundaries can offer us a sense of being grounded, something we can put our feet on when we are thrown off balance. Receiving this hexagram means that you need to ground yourself in some reality—now.

Being Grounded

In Chinese tradition this hexagram speaks highly of being humble and modest. To become grounded in modesty and humbleness is guaranteed to bring happiness and further success. Being humble does not mean holding yourself back; rather, it means being balanced and realistic in all that you do. Know that everything ebbs and flows and that there is a time and place for everything. This may be your time to have; next time it may be your time to go without. Being modest means that we know that all our good comes from relating to our spiritual source correctly. It does not mean in any way that we are better than someone else. When we are humble, we step back at times to let others be first in line. This does not mean we don't do our best; we simply allow room for others to express their best as well. Being humble and modest, then, is a way to be grounded.

First Line ▬▬ ▬▬

As we acquire qualities such as modesty, compassion, inner strength, and spiritual understanding, we often want to show off. It would be better to practice these qualities with others and let them witness for themselves your strength and beauty. If we get too arrogant we lose the grounding qualities that make us so likable.

Second Line ▬▬ ▬▬

The more you practice being grounded in qualities such as modesty, the more happiness you are assured. Being manipulative is quite immodest. Receiving this line means that you want to be manipulative but are thinking better of it and are instead grounding your thoughts and behaviors in modesty. Therefore, you can have a positive effect on the situation.

Third Line ▬▬▬▬▬

Oftentimes athletes in high school become disillusioned and even depressed when they enter college and their adult life and are no longer recognized for their athletic feats. Being grounded and modest means not relying solely on one quality or talent to get you through life. Being a basketball star or a chess champion is only one of a plethora of qualities one possesses. Use this time in your life to bring forth many of your positive qualities and to appreciate the many talents of other people. However, it is during this time of your life that it is also important to show off your talents to others. So being grounded doesn't mean that you have to hide your talents.

Fourth Line ▬▬ ▬▬

Enjoy the recognition that comes easily and naturally, but do not go further with it. Public opinion and popularity are in reality fleeting things. Enjoy the favoritism, while at the same time recognizing its limit. It won't likely last, and being popular isn't any kind of promise for what the future holds. Step back enough from all the attention (getting grounded) to enjoy it while not being distracted by it. This approach can make the attention last longer, and when it does end, you won't crash. Staying grounded during times of favoritism allows us to not be disappointed during more lean times.

Fifth Line ▬▬ ▬▬

This is a good time to move ahead with some plans you have been considering lately. Recruit the help of supportive people and you can make positive strides in your efforts. Others want to help you because you have practiced modesty and kindness with them.

Sixth Line ▬▬ ▬▬

Now is the time to be humble and modest in all your actions. If feelings of anger, jealousy, and arrogance are rising up within you, wait until they have been grounded in humility before taking action.

Consider

Grounding Meditation

This meditation is great for times when you feel overwhelmed or when you feel off balance (ungrounded). This meditation can be read out loud by a friend or read slowly to yourself.

Sit in a chair, your feet uncrossed and touching the floor. Gently close your eyes and bring your awareness to your breathing . . . simply notice how your body, all on its own, breathes in and breathes out. Notice the breath within the body, how it moves in and out, and rises and falls in the belly. Continue to breathe while bringing your awareness down to the bottoms of your feet.

Now, continuing to breathe, imagine roots coming out from the bottoms of your feet. Have the roots move down through the floor and through the layers of earth. Imagine this without too much effort and continue to breathe as the roots move down through all the layers of earth until they reach the center of the earth. When they reach the center of the earth, simply imagine the earth energy moving up into the roots, the roots pulling up that core earth energy. While still breathing in and out, have the earth energy move up the roots, into the bottoms of your feet, up your legs, and up into your body until it reaches your solar plexus. Fill this area entirely with this earth energy. Then imagine it moving down and out, so you have a continual circle of earth energy coming in and going out. Sit for a few minutes in this grounded energy.

Grounding hands us our life. We become the cause of our own life rather than the effect. Ungrounded, we become the effect of everything around us. Take time to ground and be in your body.
—Colleen Brenzy, intuitive healer, philosopher

Thunder above

Earth below

16

Intensity

"I can't believe that!" said Alice.
"Can't you?" the queen said in a pitying tone.
"Try again, draw a long breath, and shut your eyes."
Alice laughed. "There's no use trying," she said.
"One can't believe impossible things."
"I daresay you haven't had much practice," said the
queen. "When I was your age, I always did it for half
an hour a day. Why, sometimes I believed in as
many as six impossible things before breakfast."
—Lewis Carroll, from *Through the Looking Glass*

You are in your intense years. It is a time of life when many strong feelings, ideas, insights, and plans come to you. The years are about taking healthy risks, feeling your intensity, believing in the impossible, and nurturing the person you are to

Intensity

become. The image of this hexagram is of thunder resounding out of the earth. Your thunder, your intensity! When you receive this hexagram you are asked to honor this intensity. How are you using this energy now? Or, does it seem as if this energy is using you? This intense energy can be nourishing and creative when used correctly. Used incorrectly, it can be dangerous and harmful.

Feeling your energy and using it correctly means that you express yourself in ways that are not harmful to you or others. Is someone asking you to take a dangerous risk, or are you abusing drugs and losing a sense of purpose and direction in your life? How can you honor this energy of yours in this situation? Do you need to speak up about something? As a teenager or young adult you are meant to make others uncomfortable with your ideas and insights. You are bringing change with you as you move through your teen years. This is why you need this intense energy and why the entire community needs it as well. You are meant to disrupt the status quo with your energy and get us out of the rut we are in and into a new place. Change is the rule of life, and your intensity is meant to help you and the community change! Creative use of this intensity can open doors for you now and in the future.

First Line ▬ ▬

It is important to connect your intensity to a purpose and to your Higher Power. Without these, your intensity can become harmful and lead you down a path of regrets. If you become overly excited and pushy with your energy, negative things can result.

Second Line ▬ ▬

As soon as you realize that you are making a mistake is the time to correct matters. There are sure to be times when you use your intensity in adverse ways. If you change your direction at the moment you realize your wrongdoing, no long-term harm will come of it. As soon as you sense that something is not right, step back and consider the situation. This would be a good time to meditate and reflect on the direction you are taking. This approach can have very positive results.

Third Line ▬ ▬

Be careful not to rely on others to direct your intensity. This is how some of us get caught up in cults, gangs, or harmful romantic relationships. Others who truly respect you and your intensity should not try to take control of it in any way. Instead, they can show you how they use their energy and offer you support in using yours in creative and healthy ways.

Fourth Line ▬▬▬

Dedication to what is right and good attracts goodness into your life. Using your intensity in good ways can bring about goodness. Doors will open, and a sense of purpose and happiness is assured for those who take responsibility for their intensity.

Fifth Line ▬ ▬

Your teenage angst is getting the best of you. Although you have reason to feel angry and disappointed, you are (or are considering) going down a negative path. You are forgetting the times that you were helped by your spiritual source and that anything is possible. Take the time to open yourself again to what is possible; be patient and the hoped-for outcome can and will happen. Sometimes we misuse our intensity to insist that things go a certain way. This approach leaves out the influence of Spirit, which is not so predictable and often has a timetable different from our own.

Sixth Line ▬ ▬

Your intensity is misguided. You are moving toward a negative outcome because you hold on too tightly to negative attitudes. Correcting your attitude now will help make a positive outcome possible.

豫

Consider

If you are feeling restless-intensity try any one or all of the following suggestions.

- Write a poem and send it out to at least ten unsuspecting people in your community. Be brave enough to sign it.

- Make a drum and join a drumming group.

- Go dancing.

- Attend a rave without getting high on drugs. Take a tape recorder and tape interviews with people. Submit the interviews and your commentary to public radio.

- Sleep under the stars alone for one night.

- Find someone who offers coming-of-age rituals for teens and go through the ritual.

- Speak your mind to someone who will listen and respect you.

- Believe in at least six impossible things. Write them out in your journal to refer to later. "Impossible" things happen every day!

When thunder bursts above the Earth, myriad beings are
nourished by its yang energy and become delighted and alive.
**—Taoist Master Alfred Huang,
from *The Complete I Ching,* hexagram 16**

Lake above

Thunder below

17

Getting What You Want

You already possess everything necessary to become great.
—Crow proverb,
from *The Soul Would Have No Rainbow*

This may be a time when you are trying to get others to agree with you on something. If we want others to agree with us, we need to have a strong sense of our own beliefs and what it is we want. When we are strong in our own principles and act on our own inner truth, others may follow us. The longer you follow your own inner truth and work at living the principles offered in the I Ching, others will easily and naturally listen to and agree with you.

Right now, whatever the circumstances, practice *acceptance* and following the good within yourself, even if circumstances continue to get worse. Following the good can bring events around in time to benefit you. Although at this time others

may not be in agreement with you, they may come to understand and support your opinion. They may do this because you have respected them by accepting their position. Getting others to agree with you can be a very challenging task. It is best to help them *understand* what it is you want from them or the situation. When you focus on understanding each other, rather than forcing someone to agree with you, a good outcome is assured. In all healthy relationships it is good to build in the "agreement to disagree." This means we accept that those close to us won't always be in agreement with us, and vice versa.

When we go into any discussions, we first have to have an understanding of our own truths, then we need to focus on understanding the other person's view, while agreeing to disagree. With this approach others are sure to listen to you and follow your suggestions. What we find out is that we don't really have to agree on everything to get the support and involvement of others.

First Line ━━━━

Remain open to others who are disagreeing with you or taking another path. If you are trying to influence them, this openness and gentleness toward them can help. Remember, remaining open does not mean that you abandon your beliefs and principles; it means that you stay strong in your own principles while being open to the choices and views of others.

Second Line ━━ ━━

You are getting impatient with others or unfavorable circumstances, and this impatience is turning into hostility. You may want to try to force things, but this can only make the situation worse. Follow the good within yourself and don't push; this can bring the best outcome possible in this situation. As you demonstrate a genuine desire to follow your truth, others will come to your side when you most need them.

Third Line ━━ ━━

There are times when it can be very challenging to do what we know is correct. This is one of those times. On the one hand, you want to prove yourself to others. On the other hand, you know this doesn't feel right to you. Follow the good and good will follow you. Hang in there, and things will work out.

Fourth Line ━━━━

Learning to follow the good within yourself gets others to follow and understand you.

Fifth Line ━━━━

Keep following what you know to be correct and true, even when you are tempted to give up. This guarantees great success and you are developing a strong character that will help you your entire life.

Sixth Line ━━ ━━

You are encouraged to focus on the needs of the moment instead of worrying about the future. Also, if you are having difficulty, ask your spiritual source for help through this time.

Consider

Identify someone with whom you are in disagreement, someone you care about. Practice the following three steps to encourage others to understand you, which can lead them to agree with you.

1   Have a good understanding of your own thoughts, feelings, and beliefs (your inner truth).

2. Make the purpose of the conversation to *understand* your friend's point of view. While listening, remind yourself that it is okay to disagree. The goal here is to understand the other person's point of view.

3. Once you have listened and the other person knows that you understand him or her, can you come to some sort of agreement about the issue? It may be to simply agree that you disagree. This difference of opinion can be celebrated, because no two people think and feel exactly alike. What you discover in time is that all we really want is to be heard and understood; being agreed with is secondary.

Mountain above

Wind below

18

Mend What Is Broken

How can I be useful; of what service can I be?
There is something inside me; what can it be?
—Vincent van Gogh, artist

All the world is full of suffering; it is also full of overcoming it.
—Helen Keller, lecturer on behalf of the blind

During our teen years, and the entire journey into adulthood, we are extra sensitive to all that is not right around us. We know what is lost and broken in our families, in our communities, and on the planet. It hurts us and at times overwhelms us to see people and the planet suffering so much. You can be part of the mending of what is broken, if you choose. In fact, many cultures believe that those in their teens have the intense energy needed to help heal what is broken—to help us start again.

Receiving this hexagram is a sign that there is something broken within your reach, which you can help mend. This could be something within yourself, a friend or family member, or in society at large. It could be a problem you've identified within your school or work environment. Your duty now is to think about what action you can take to effect positive change in this fractured area. Most likely, the problem is old and can take time and commitment to improve. Don't give up. You may or may not be able to see the full results of your efforts, but taking action can make a positive difference.

There is a saying that "if you are not part of the solution, you are part of the problem." This is true in this case. Since you have identified something that needs mending, it is your responsibility now to be part of the healing process. Know that your efforts can benefit you and many others affected by the problem. If you are wondering whether or not you should speak up about a concern, receiving this hexagram indicates that, yes, it is time to speak up.

The changing lines offer more insight to particular areas that may need mending.

First Line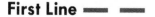

You have acquired some "broken behaviors" that originate from your family's values and traditions. For example, your parents abuse alcohol, as did their parents. Now you are starting to abuse alcohol. Another example is how your family relates to others: a "broken" tradition is one in which a family views itself as better or above others. What broken family values are you still holding on to that need to be changed?

Second Line ━━━

You are resistant to knowing the truth. The truth is likely something you fear, knowing that it may mean change once you become more aware of the problem. Your fear is not legitimate: you can handle the change that needs to take place to improve the situation. Step back and take another look at the issue, trusting yourself, because you are strong enough to deal with it.

Third Line ━━━

You may have overreacted to a situation. Rest assured that this overreaction is better than not taking any action at all. Stay involved, but relax your efforts.

Fourth Line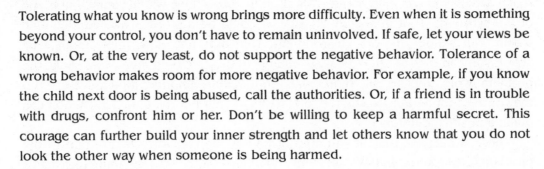

Tolerating what you know is wrong brings more difficulty. Even when it is something beyond your control, you don't have to remain uninvolved. If safe, let your views be known. Or, at the very least, do not support the negative behavior. Tolerance of a wrong behavior makes room for more negative behavior. For example, if you know the child next door is being abused, call the authorities. Or, if a friend is in trouble with drugs, confront him or her. Don't be willing to keep a harmful secret. This courage can further build your inner strength and let others know that you do not look the other way when someone is being harmed.

Fifth Line

There are times when others try to make you feel obliged to accept a wrong way of doing things. You are never obliged to anyone in this way, even when this person holds authority over you. Live by what you know to be right and correct.

Sixth Line

Withdrawal from negative influences at this time is the right thing to do. Once you remove yourself from the situation, focus on mending yourself and not judging others. They err because they have not yet become aware that what they do is wrong.

Consider

Throughout our lives we need to begin things again and again. When we are willing to start over, we can then let go of old hurts and start fresh with one another. Such an approach and willingness to start over in our intimate relationships can create an enduring bond. The willingness to start over can help in all areas of our lives: school, friendships, any project we are having difficulty with. Being able to start over, and approach ourselves and others with fresh ideas, makes change easier.

What needs a fresh start in your life? Where do you need to start over?

What would help you have a fresh attitude toward an old activity or relationship?

Earth above

Lake below

19

Something Approaches

Before enlightenment, I chopped wood and carried water; after enlightenment, I chopped wood and carried water.
—Zen saying

Receiving this hexagram alerts you to the approach of powerful and beneficial events. All movement in your life is toward improvement and growth. Much growth and change are at hand, and it is possible because you have prepared for this through your efforts and your relationship with Spirit. It is important to respond positively and quickly to this time of approaching opportunity. Do not postpone or procrastinate, or the opportunity that approaches may pass and be missed. How you use these times of opportunity influences how things will turn out.

When we take on a healthy attitude during times of opportunity, we benefit fully. But when we relax too much and forget to keep our focus on the spiritual path and principles, we miss the opportunity. Continue to be balanced and humble as the opportunity comes into fruition. Be kind, patient, and generous to those less fortunate than you. Doing so can bring further success.

First Line ━━━━━━

Be conscientious and cautious in your initial response to these good times. Use the opportunity while being careful not to overextend yourself. It would be like spending the winnings of a lottery ticket before you received the money, only to find out that several others won the lottery too. So, enjoy the good times with some caution.

Second Line ━━━━━━

Rely on your spiritual source to help you through the present difficulty. You simply may be feeling overwhelmed. Spirit knows how to make good from even the most challenging times.

Third Line ━━ ━━

You are about to lapse into some negative behaviors, such as belittling others, showing off to someone who will be hurt by this, or gossiping. Be careful, and catch yourself the moment you begin to engage in such thoughts or behaviors and good will result.

Fourth Line ━━ ━━

Can you disagree with someone while remaining open to them? Can you focus on the other person's abilities, even though you may be in disagreement about something? If you can, this may benefit both of you.

Fifth Line ━━ ━━

The I Ching counsels us that we cannot truly succeed without the help of our Higher Power (the "Creative"). Doing something on our own is not at the exclusion of our Higher Power. Lasting happiness and success come from having an ongoing relationship with our spiritual source. As good times approach, keep in mind the role your Higher Power had in making this success.

Sixth Line ━━ ━━

When you practice love and compassion toward yourself and others, that is what you will experience in return. Great and lasting happiness comes to those who act out of love and compassion.

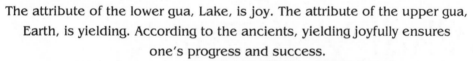

Consider

Imagine that someone has sent you $10,000 to spend as you wish. How would you spend this money? Journal your response.

A few days later, when you have time, review your journal entry. Is there anything you would change? Is there something or someone you left out when considering how you would spend this money? What has changed from the initial response to now, and what brought about this change of mind?

The attribute of the lower gua, Lake, is joy. The attribute of the upper gua, Earth, is yielding. According to the ancients, yielding joyfully ensures one's progress and success.

—Taoist Master Alfred Huang,
from *The Complete I Ching*, hexagram 19

20

You Really Are What You Think

You must give birth to your images. They are the future waiting to be born.
—Rainer Maria Rilke, German poet

A basic truth about ourselves is that we become that on which we fix our attention. Therefore, as we study, practice, and meditate on the principles of the I Ching, these principles become reflected in our attitudes, energy, and relationships. When we think about the possibilities of positive outcomes, for example, this makes room for positive possibilities. Ideally, the I Ching encourages us to keep an open mind— one that allows room for many possible situations. This allows us to be more present for the moment, because we remain open to the potential of each situation.

How we think about something directly affects what kind of experience we will have. What is your mind focused on? How do you perceive things? There is a joke that goes something like this: An optimist perceives the glass half full, the pessimist perceives the glass half empty, while the scientist sees that the glass is simply too big. Each person's thought in this case affects how he or she feels and reacts to the situation.

Receiving this hexagram means that you need to step back from your thoughts and perceptions. Are you engaging in correct thinking? Are you caught up in some negative thoughts or assumptions? When you anticipate the future, are you open to all possibilities or do you just offer yourself one possibility? Is the glass half full, or do you simply need to get a smaller glass?

It is important to take time to train your mind—to have some command of your own thoughts. And this is quite possible. In Tibetan Buddhism this practice is called Lojong; the mind is trained to focus on principles such as loving-kindness, openness, acceptance, and patience. Ultimately, all the hexagrams within the I Ching guide you to use your mind creatively and wisely. There are many books available on positive thinking and how this dramatically improves life, including the following: *Start Where You Are* by Pema Chödrön (Boston: Shambhala, 1994); *The Wisdom of No Escape* by Pema Chödrön (Boston: Shambhala, 1991); *The Four Agreements* by don Miguel Ruiz (San Rafael, Calif.: Amber-Allen, 1997); *The Four Agreements Companion Book* by don Miguel Ruiz (San Rafael, Calif.: Amber-Allen, 2000); and *The 7 Habits of Highly Effective Teens* by Stephen Covey (New York: Fireside, 1998).

First Line ▬▬ ▬▬

Not everyone you know may recognize the benefits of following truths such as those offered through the I Ching. By deepening your own conviction to truths such as compassion and inner independence, you will have a positive influence on others and encourage them to follow your example.

Second Line ▬▬ ▬▬

Do not take the negative situation personally or to heart. The love and wisdom of your Higher Power is present in this situation and will guide you. Be patient, and this time of ambiguity can flower into something good. This is a good opportunity to practice not taking others' behaviors and comments personally. What others say and do is a reflection of them, not you.

Third Line ▬ ▬

Things are not as they appear, so don't get too caught up in the appearance of events. Outside circumstances are not as problematic as they seem. By working on cultivating healthy thoughts, you can come up with a favorable solution.

Fourth Line ▬ ▬

When you apply the principles taught in the I Ching to every situation, the overall suffering in the world decreases. Any time you work on improving yourself, you add to the peace and beauty of all. In Navajo tradition this is called walking the beauty way. Indigenous peoples understand that everything we do, even our thoughts, affects everyone.

Walking the Beauty Way

The Spiritual Warrior's journey to beauty is a journey both to self and to Spirit. It is a path of choice. When you walk in beauty (loving thoughts and generous acts) you manifest a life of beauty. In the journey of the Beauty Way in the Navajo tradition it is understood that once you achieve this beauty (love, peace of mind, a connection to Spirit) you can bring this into the world through your positive beliefs and loving actions. You are then walking in the Beauty Way. For more on this, read *Navajo and Tibetan Sacred Wisdom: The Circle of the Spirit* by Peter Gold (Rochester, Vt.: Inner Traditions, 1994).

Fifth Line ▬▬▬

Take the time to step back from the situation and reflect. Reflect on your own thoughts and assumptions. Doing so can bring forth superior and beneficial qualities within you. Focus on the qualities you want to develop in yourself and know that this can bring about good results.

Sixth Line ━━━

Everyone makes mistakes. This is just proof of our humanity. It is what you do with your mistakes that develops your character. Use the mistake as an opportunity, and an opportunity may present itself.

觀

> ● *Consider* ●
>
> For one day, every hour on the hour, ask yourself: What is it that my mind is focused on? Take a moment to bring your awareness to your thoughts and what your attention is on. How is this thought affecting the way you feel and act at the moment? How often do you find yourself caught up in negative thoughts? How often are positive thoughts directing you?

A fundamental fact of consciousness is that we take on the attributes and energy of that upon which we focus our attention.
—**Brian Browne Walker, from *The I Ching or Book of Changes: A Guide to Life's Turning Points***

嗜

嗑

21
Removing Obstacles

*This is a world of action, and not for moping and
groaning in.*
—Charles Dickens, English novelist

*You must be the change you wish to see in the
world.*
—Mahatma Gandhi, Indian nationalist and spiritual leader

Force is at times necessary to remove obstacles. The force of honesty, courage, and
perseverance is what is called for here. This hexagram is about forcing through an
obstacle so that unity can happen between you and others or you and your spiritual
source. Something is between you and another (or others), and it is up to you to use
force to get through the obstacle. You might need courage to get through some hard
feelings or lack of forgiveness before you can connect with another person. You

should use force with the *obstacle,* not the other person. For example, you may hold a longtime grudge against someone. In order to have a relationship with this person, you need to force yourself through the grudge. This will take courage on your part.

It is always scary to let go of a grudge or belief we have held on to for so long. This is because we have become so attached to it that we are not sure how things will go when we no longer hold it. Therefore, we need some force to break through the hold this belief has on us.

Oftentimes it is a level of comfort that we need to force ourselves through: "I have always done it this way, so I always will." But there is a saying that "if you always do what you always did, you will always get what you always got." So, if you want *new* and *better* results, move through the obstacle by doing things differently.

First Line

Learn from the mistake the first time, when possible. Repeating the same mistake only exacerbates the problem. Sometimes it is simply a matter of *admitting* that we are making a mistake, and then changing course. Can you admit that you may have made a mistake?

Second Line ▬▬ ▬▬

Your judgment of someone else's wrongdoing has gone too far. It is important to realize when someone else is causing harm and to let him or her know it is wrong. But to continue to hold that person in a negative light is going too far.

Third Line ▬▬ ▬▬

A matter that keeps coming up for you with others has surfaced once again. Wanting to get even or punish the other person will only create more problems. Use force to get to the bottom of the matter and how it relates to *you,* and take your focus off trying to force the other person to change. Change yourself and things will eventually work out.

Fourth Line ▬▬▬

In order for things to work out you need to use your force to get through the problem. Be strong and firm in dealing with the issue. You may also be strong and firm in dealing with other people, but don't let this turn into harshness toward them. The best way to get through this is to practice self-control. All great people master the art of self-control.

Fifth Line ━━ ━━

Continue to remain strong and independent of the wrongdoing. Can you at the same time have kind and gentle thoughts toward this person to whom you are estranged? Focus on your inner independence, because your Higher Power is correcting the situation. Harmony with this person will take place in time.

Sixth Line ━━━━

When you become inflexible, and are not considering others, you end up demeaning yourself. You need to soften your stubbornness and open yourself to other possibilities. This line may also mean that you are dealing with someone else who is obstinate. You can't force him or her to change; instead, just go on your own way.

Consider

Make contact with a friend who you know cares about you, and who has known you for a while. Ask that person to write a letter to you about all the traits and accomplishments he or she admires in you. This can give you the support to move through the obstacle(s) that is (are) before you now.

Mountain above

Fire below

22

Beauty and the Beast

Go confidently in the direction of your dreams! Live the life you've imagined. As you simplify your life, the laws of the universe will be simpler.
—Henry David Thoreau, American essayist, naturalist, and author of *Walden*

This hexagram suggests that you bring forth the qualities of beauty and grace in this situation. Bringing such qualities into our lives allows us to deal with the beastly things that show up in life. Bring forth your own natural beauty, and it will be brought out in others. This natural beauty is often called our True Nature. Our True Nature has all the qualities of grace, beauty, and strength that are mentioned throughout the I Ching. It is our deepest desire to bring forth this True Nature. But all of us have a beast to deal with first. The beast in us conceals our True Nature. This part is usually aggressive, pushy, and afraid—just like the beast in the fairy tale *Beauty and the Beast.* It tries to use intimidation to make others do what it wants. The beast in us usually just scares people or puts them off; then we find we are alone and isolated from others. Qualities within us or outside circumstances that are beastly can be won over through the power of beauty and grace.

Receiving this hexagram also means that the beauty and grace in this situation have won or are about to win over the beast. A difficulty has passed and changed into a time of beauty and grace. This is so because you have let some of your True Nature, your beauty, come forth.

First Line ━━━━━

Try not to bully another person to get your way. Especially in the beginning of relationships or projects, don't try to push things along. Be open to what others are bringing to the table, and accept that you don't have all the answers. This is also a good time to open yourself to the help of your Higher Power through prayer.

What Is a Prayer?

A prayer is a request put out to our Higher Power, to the spirit world, asking for help and support. It is a "call" for the spirit world to intervene in our affairs. Knowing that we are being heard and that a response is inevitable, we could include a statement of gratitude. A prayer can include a request for the best possible outcome for all concerned, because Spirit wants this for all of us.

Second Line ━━ ━━

Underneath the mean exterior of the beast is a handsome prince. This line encourages you to try to see beyond the appearances and into the truth of the situation or person. In reality, a person could be a handsome prince (or beautiful princess) on the *outside* and a beast within! Take the necessary time to see the truth.

Third Line ━━━

Circumstances and others appear okay, but remain cautious. Do not relax too much, or assume too much too quickly. If you maintain a conscientious and reserved attitude things can work out. This means that you hold full judgment and trust of the situation or person because more needs to be revealed to you.

Fourth Line ━━ ━━

Wanting to rush things or prove yourself can bring trouble. A return to the qualities of beauty and grace can prevent disaster.

Fifth Line ━━ ━━

You want to be recognized for something, but if you get too pushy about this it will only make things worse. You will be recognized and rewarded if you let go of *having* to be popular or recognized. Receiving this line may mean that you are dealing with others to whom popularity is of great importance. Deal with them gracefully, for they don't realize how beastly they are behaving.

Sixth Line ━━━

By bringing forth the qualities of beauty and grace, you have won over the beastly situation and obtained inner strength. Your True Nature is shining through!

Consider

Watch a video of an original *Beauty and the Beast* production or attend the play. Notice how it is that Beauty wins over and helps the Beast. Consider how this fairy tale is about each of our journeys to bring forth our own True Nature. What beastly qualities do you need to release in order to allow your Beauty to come forward?

Mountain above

Earth below

23

Falling Apart without Losing It

We think that the point is to pass the test or to overcome the problem, but the truth is that things don't really get solved. They come together and they fall apart. Then they come together again and fall apart again. It's just like that. The healing comes from letting there be room for all of this to happen: room for grief, for relief, for misery, for joy.
—Pema Chödrön, Buddhist nun, from *When Things Fall Apart*

There are times throughout our lives when things just seem to fall apart—such times cannot be avoided. This is one of those times for you. There are likely many

forces occurring now, pressing on you from all sides. Perhaps people are making demands of you or are arguing with you or with each other. A lot around you is at odds. When adversity strikes us like this, we usually feel compelled to act and do something about it. We worry that if we don't do something quickly, we will lose control. We become filled with doubt and anxiety. We often forget to rely on the help of our spiritual source and lose hope that things can work out.

The key here is to fall apart without losing it. Don't lose hope or inner independence; don't lose your focus on your spiritual path. Take no action toward others. Go nowhere; make no big decisions until this time has passed. Instead, focus on practicing your spiritual principles, accept that such times of adversity happen to us all, and weather the difficulty with patience. Use this time for reflection and gathering insight and courage. Not acting rashly can take a lot of courage. We feel compelled to make *something* happen. Letting go and being still shows Spirit we trust in its wisdom and help.

Receiving this hexagram may also mean that it is time for you and a friend to part. Every relationship changes, and many throughout our teen years come to an end. Accept that during these years you will have both long-term and short-term relationships. This is quite natural. Can you let go of relationships with acceptance and kindness, wishing the other person well?

First Line ▬ ▬

Fear and doubt are taking over. You feel you have to act. You need to focus on letting go of your anger and gripes. This does not mean that you don't have reason to feel angry, but acting on these feelings at this time will only increase the difficulty.

Second Line ▬ ▬

Trouble is all around you. If you remain stubborn and insistent, things will only become more difficult and painful for you. Do not hold on to silent anger with attitudes such as "I don't care." Such hostile emotions will only burden you more. Be still and wait on the power of Spirit to help you. Seek the support of those you trust.

Third Line ▬ ▬

You are successful at backing away from difficulty, even though you still are struggling with intense feelings. This stepping back allows you to experience the help of your Higher Power. Those who may be trying to hurt you have little effect on you now.

Fourth Line ━━ ━━

The situation has gotten as bad as it is going to get. It has reached its peak. Continue to remain still and strong and place your attention on your feelings and attitude: Are you holding on to a grudge? Are you thinking of trying to make something happen? What are you afraid will happen? Are you letting in the help of Spirit?

Fifth Line ━━ ━━

The great person does not make excuses or blame others for his or her surrounding difficulties. Recognize your own faults and try to improve your attitude instead of trying to change others. Succeeding at this helps turn things around favorably.

Sixth Line ━━━━

You are having difficulty letting go of the situation and are tending to hold on to negative and harmful attitudes. Therefore, events worsen. It is time to get away from the problem and reflect on your attitude. Such reflection can help you realize how your attitude can affect the situation. A return to a more pleasant time is slow. However, if you take this time to reflect on your feelings and attitude, you will have made much progress and can find the needed support from others.

Remember to reflect on yourself with compassion and kindness. This isn't about beating up on yourself but about gaining perspective about your own feelings and attitude. Be kind to yourself.

Consider

The image that goes with this hexagram is one of a mountain sitting on the earth. Have you ever visited a mountain and sat on its slope? It sits powerful and still while ants, lions, coyotes, deer, ticks, and poisonous snakes move and live on its great body. It sits still as storms and winds and changing seasons beat upon its green and brown belly. *Nothing disturbs a mountain.* This is a time for you to be large and unmovable, like a mountain. Let the snakes of adversity run about you and winds of change blow at you while you remain strong, still, and grand. You too will survive this adversity like a mountain.

Earth above

Thunder below

24

A Turning Point

Winter solitude—
In a world of one color
The sound of wind.
—Basho, Japanese haiku poet

You have come to a turning point; the greatest difficulty is over and better times approach. However, you are not to rush the process; let it take its *natural* course. This time of change will take as long as needed for things to work out. This is a good time to gather energy and rest, much like many plants and animals do in the wintertime, knowing that this stored energy will be used when spring arrives.

It is time to turn toward the good within yourself and consider what gifts, traits, and ideas are gathering energy inside of you. Reflect on your goodness. Your gifts and talents are part of your True Nature and want to come out and express themselves. Whereas there is a time of action, now is the time of being with yourself and your ideas. Life will offer you many opportunities to express yourself, because there has been a place made for all that you have to offer the world. Just as the seed holds within it the potential of the plant it is to become, or as the empty canvas awaits the painter, you now hold the potential for your future.

First Line ━━━━

You may have deviated from what you thought was right. If you return to what is correct, no harm will come to you or others.

Second Line ━━ ━━

You are ready to give up on negative thoughts and return to a more positive attitude.

Third Line ━━ ━━

Sometimes we continue to make the same mistakes. Is this happening now with you? We often keep repeating mistakes until we learn the lesson offered to us by the difficulty. What lesson keeps repeating itself in your life?

Fourth Line ━━ ━━

You may be associating with those who have had a negative influence on you but are now ready to take a better path. Who you share your time with has a huge impact on your life. Your ability to end harmful relationships brings positive changes for you.

Fifth Line ━━ ━━

Try not to be hard on yourself for any mistakes you made. Such mistakes are simply part of the learning process. They give you a better idea of what works for you and what doesn't. Once you realize the mistake, correct it and move on.

Sixth Line ━━ ━━

Pay attention to the time in your life when events transition. This is a vulnerable time. Be careful not to give in to negative ideas. Rest and focus on your inner strengths, and everything can return to the good.

Consider

Include in your morning meditation the following prayer. This is intended to illicit loving-kindness for you and for others. Say it to yourself several times, allowing the feelings and ideas to fill your body and mind.

> May I be filled with loving-kindness.
> May I be well.
> May I be at peace.
> May all my dreams come true.

Then send these thoughts out to all others:

> May you be filled with loving-kindness.
> May you be well.
> May you be happy.
> May you be at peace.
> May all your dreams come true.

For more on loving-kindness, refer to Sharon Salzberg's book *Loving-Kindness: The Revolutionary Art of Happiness* (Boston: Shambhala, 1995).

We are the doorway through which life unfolds.

—Wu Wei, I Ching scholar,
from *I Ching Wisdom*, volume II

25

Truth

To believe in God or in a guiding force because someone tells you to is the height of stupidity. We are given senses to receive our information with. With our own eyes we see, and with our skin we feel. With our intelligence, it is intended that we understand. But each person must puzzle it out for himself or herself.

—Sophy Burnham, American novelist

Sometimes your friends are wrong. Sometimes they are right. The truth about this situation, as most, exists within you. The I Ching wants to guide you to this Inner Truth, so such truth may always be available to you. No one else can fully explain the truth to you—we each have to discover it for ourselves. This Inner Truth is an expression of our True Nature, which is always connected to our spiritual source.

No matter what the difficulty, holding on to what is true for you can help you get through it. Truth is the one constant through all the changes in our lives, leading to positive solutions. In contrast, something that is not true leads to more problems. Inner truth is connected to cosmic truth. For example, it is my personal truth to not steal anything. The cosmic law of cause and effect (karma) supports this personal truth. Knowing your own truths and living by them can only strengthen you. Each hexagram within the I Ching strives to lead you to your own personal truths, something for you to discover and figure out for yourself. The I Ching will not give you rules; rather, it guides you along your own path.

Receiving this hexagram means that you need to open your mind to your own truths and live by what you believe to be true. Be curious about the truth in this and every situation, but find your own truth. Be careful not to "look aside" for your answers. This means that you shouldn't compare yourself to others. When we compare ourselves to others we lose touch with our Inner Truth and end up responding to what we think others expect of us. We are all unique and at different stages of our development; comparing is therefore futile.

First Line

Remember: within each of us lives a divine spirit, our True Nature. When you access this, good can only follow.

Second Line ━━ ━━

Too often you are caught up in the outcome. You become overly concerned about the results instead of doing things for the sake of doing them. Let go of what might happen, and all will go well. Keep your focus on the path, and let go of the goal. Focusing on the path can get you to a desired goal.

Third Line ━━ ━━

You have encountered undeserved problems. Negative things that are not your fault happen. It is best to not get too upset; instead, do what you need to do to take care of yourself. Getting caught up in the problem may result in more misfortune. Don't let such negative events take you away from your Inner Truth.

Fourth Line ━━━

Fear and dread of losing are just as harmful as wanting too much to win. Do not be swayed by such extremes, either of your own making or others. Remain open to what is possible—letting go of the extremes.

Fifth Line ━━━

The trouble can pass on its own. Do not try to fix it, and it will pass quickly.

Sixth Line ━━━

When you try too hard to force events, you are not relying on the truth to get you through. Go with your initial idea and then let things progress naturally to the next stage. We get in the way of Spirit's help when we feel we have to push and shove our way to the goal.

Consider

What truths do you live by, and how can you connect this to more cosmic truths? Cosmic truths are truths that are real to us all. And when we are in alignment with these cosmic truths we are in a state of grace with the universe and our spiritual source. Can you identify several personal truths that are in alignment with cosmic truth?

The ancient sages considered thunder to be the sound of Heaven. The thunder rolling under Heaven proclaimed these virtues to myriad beings. Those who preserved and nurtured these virtues were naturally aligned with the will of Heaven and would be powerful and endowed with the potential to be successful.

—Taoist Master Alfred Huang,
from *The Complete I Ching*, hexagram 25

Mountain above

Heaven below

26
Practice under Fire

What is to give light must endure burning.
**—Vicktor Frankl, Viennese psychiatrist
and author of *Man's Search for Meaning***

You and your spiritual principles are under fire. This is a time to hold firm to what you know to be true. It may be one simple truth, such as "be kind" or "don't take it personally." Stand strong and silent as the fire builds around you. Somebody may be attempting to throw you off center. Embody the lessons and wisdom you have acquired through your use of the I Ching, and you will get through this successfully.

Ultimately such times become times of opportunity for you to practice your spiritual skills. If life were all chocolates and roses we wouldn't have anything to practice with! We can't learn and grow if we live in a room with all the doors closed, and we never go outside. But then when we do open the doors, someone who really gets on our nerves walks in and takes the best seat! So what do you do? What principles can you apply when some false rumor about you is being passed around at school? What principles can you use when it seems you have lost favor with someone, or everyone? What principles can you apply when you have decided to say no to something all your friends are saying yes to (and now they are teasing you)?

Others will test your abilities to stick to your principles. When this happens, keep still (don't get into defending yourself), hold firm (focus on what you know is right), and hold together (be kind to yourself and remember to accept the help of Spirit). In doing this you will eventually have a positive influence on others and the situation. Others will trust your strength and character because you endure challenging times by holding firm to your principles.

First Line ━━━━

You are tempted to react to the offensive situation, but stand firm. You are getting hooked and are beginning to be carried away by other people's negativity. Their behaviors may make you feel as if you *have* to fight back. This will not help you. Endure the difficulty and things will work out. Get hooked by the negativity and the offensive situation will worsen.

Second Line ━━━━

Struggling with the people and circumstances that oppose you now will only make matters worse. Do your best to accept the situation and remain still. This then conserves your strength for a time when it will be more beneficial to act.

Third Line ━━━━

Difficulties force you to face your greatest fears and doubts. What fears and doubts are coming up for you at this time? Possibilities will open up for you when you are able to face these fears and doubts and learn to overcome them. Remember: most fears are based on lies such as "something bad always happens to me" or "nothing ever turns out right for me."

Fourth Line ━━ ━━

When you are caught up in strong emotions, it's dangerous and often foolish to react. Wait until these intense feelings pass. Be still, and in this stillness you will find the best way to respond to the situation. An opportunity will open to you.

Fifth Line ━━ ━━

Sometimes we can get so caught up in wanting something that we lose sight of everything else. Try to focus your thoughts on other things—other plans, relationships, and pleasures. Even better, engage in a fun activity and let go of the problem for a while.

Sixth Line ━━━━

The difficulty is removed. Meet this opening with awareness of what principles helped you achieve this victory. Did waiting and holding firm to your principles help you? Continue bringing in such principles and the success will continue.

Consider

Imagine that you are standing strong and steadfast on an ocean beach. As you stand firm and still a large and powerful wave crests and covers you completely. It is strong and forceful, but you remain **unmoved** by its power. It simply rushes over you and then washes away to the great sea as you remain standing, strong and calm. Think of this wave as the difficulty rushing over you, covering you completely, but then falling away back into the ocean as you remain unmoved and standing firm.

Every time the negative situation arises, feel the wave, feel your feet planted in the sand, and feel your firmness and strength.

This difficult time will pass, just as the wave returns to the ocean. And you will remain unharmed as long as you stand firm and still.

Mountain above

Thunder below

27
Food for the Soul

The light that lives in the sun,
Lighting all the world,
The light of the moon,
The light that is in fire:
Know that light to be mine.
—Bhagavad-Gita

This hexagram is all about how and what we "feed" ourselves and others. The food we eat, the thoughts we have, the people we associate with, and the ways we entertain ourselves are all about food for the mind, body, and soul. What we watch on television or read feeds our mind. Who we associate with feeds our soul. What we think about feeds our mind and soul. And, what we feed our body affects our soul in the same way that what we feed our mind affects our body. So, receiving this hexagram means that you need to check your "diet" and how this diet affects you and your relationships.

How well are you nourishing your developing body? What foods do you frequently eat? How well are you nourishing your mind? What thoughts are you feeding yourself? These thoughts affect the state of your mind just as the food you eat affects your physical health. How well are you feeding your soul? Soul food includes your having a connection to your life's purpose, compassion for yourself and others, and a tolerant attitude. All these are necessary for a well-fed soul.

Meditation is good food for the mind, body, and soul. Sitting still in silence for just five minutes a day can help us detoxify our heart and mind and help the body relax. And, meditation quiets us enough so that we can hear the wisdom of our spiritual source. Such a practice makes room for nourishing feelings and thoughts. Once we start to nourish ourselves, our health and circumstances begin to heal and get strong.

The I Ching counsels us not to feed ourselves on fantasy. Fantasy is the "when I win the lottery . . ." mentality. Fantasy, unlike our creative imagination, is not grounded in reality. We may get high on marijuana and fantasize about all the things we are going to do "when . . ." and never really succeed. Instead, feed yourself on reality, on "everything which is natural which is infinite which is yes . . ."

First Line ▬▬

Doubt is toxic to the mind. Doubting yourself, the potential of others, and Spirit's influence only brings on negative feelings of hopelessness. Receiving this line indicates that you may be annoyed and judgmental of others and are beginning to doubt the counsel of the I Ching. You have thought about giving up. If you practice sitting quietly, focusing on love and goodwill for others and yourself, you can uplift the situation.

Second Line ▬▬ ▬▬

Consider with whom you are associating. If you realize that you have aligned yourself with an individual or a group that is not healthy, a continued relationship with that person or group will bring you adversity. Choose your relationships carefully.

Third Line ▬▬ ▬▬

Be careful what thoughts you are harboring. Are you convincing yourself of something that is a lie? Like all people, you can be very convincing and sell yourself on ideas and behaviors that are harmful. This line counsels you that true and lasting happiness cannot be achieved through the sole pursuit of pleasure or through the abuse of mind-altering substances. Be honest with yourself about your choices. Are you over–doing something? Return to a healthier path before too much damage has occurred.

Fourth Line ━━ ━━

By feeding your mind, body, and soul well, you attract to you healthy people who support this lifestyle. The effort you have put into nourishing yourself results in happiness.

Fifth Line ━━ ━━

Feeding yourself with wholesome substances is more and more your responsibility, even if you are living in a home where others neglect themselves. It takes a special courage and commitment on your part to do what you know is best even when those around you are choosing otherwise. Spirit will step in and support your efforts to live a healthy and dynamic life.

Sixth Line ━━━━

The soul needs regular and vital nourishment. When you succeed in nourishing your soul, you are creating a life of happiness and love. Others will be affected by your well-fed soul and want to be with you. Many blessings are yours as you continue to feed your soul and the souls of others.

Consider

Change one simple habit a day for a week. For example, if you always sleep in in the morning, get out of bed ten minutes earlier each morning. If you always take the bus to school or work, ride your bike or walk with a friend. If you never eat lunch out, eat lunch out. If you never talk with your mother about your day, visit with her about your day.

Challenging our habits can help us better nourish ourselves. We tend to get into a certain groove and don't even notice what we are missing until we change what we do. As you can see by the examples above, changing just a small habit can affect what you are feeding yourself.

Beware! Change brings change!

What's Nourishing You?

There was once a young woman who constantly felt disappointed every time she spent time with her aunt. She loved her aunt, but in truth her aunt was an unkind woman who didn't really like being around young people. This young woman consulted an older friend who suggested that she "stop going to the hardware store for fruit salad." The young woman asked, "What do you mean?" "I mean that you are expecting to get something from your aunt that she cannot (or will not) give you. And nothing you do can change this. Changing yourself doesn't alter the fact that if you go in to a hardware store for anything other than hardware, you are going to be disappointed."

The young woman thought about this and realized that she would not set herself up for disappointment (this she could change!). She would just spend a little time with her aunt now and then and go to others for the more intimate experience she had hoped to have with her aunt. As a result, the girl feels less disappointment and knows where she can go for her "fruit salad." She is finding her nourishment in better places.

```
▬▬▬    ▬▬▬
▬▬▬▬▬▬▬▬▬
▬▬▬▬▬▬▬▬▬
▬▬▬▬▬▬▬▬▬
▬▬▬▬▬▬▬▬▬
▬▬▬    ▬▬▬
```

Lake above

Wind below

大

28

Extraordinary Times

过

*I walk out; I see something, some event that would
otherwise have been utterly missed and lost; or
something sees me, some enormous power
brushes me with its clean wing, and I resound like a
beaten bell.*
—Annie Dillard, author of *Pilgrim at Tinker Creek*

This is a time of great potential. Many things are possible. There are times in life when the door of opportunity swings wide open, and this is such a time. Moreover, this door opens into a vast open space, making room for dreams to come true. You can feel the energy of this potential. In fact, this energy can be quite frequent during the coming-of-age years, the years that lead into the adult years.

How you make use of this energy and potential will determine what comes of it. There is a responsibility that comes with such times, and you can feel almost burdened with the choices that need to be made. The pressures right now are great, and you can be tempted to make light of the situation or push things to a painful conclusion. People make light of such potential because we think we can't handle it. We tend to push things along because we have a difficult time letting things take their natural course, which often is slower than we prefer. But if we simply open ourselves up to the potential without pushing things, we will experience great results.

You do have what it takes to make full use of all the potential of this extraordinary time. In many ways you have been preparing for it. The I Ching recommends that you approach such extraordinary times with inner independence, patience, modesty, groundedness, and humility. The changing lines offer more guidance on particular challenges you face during such a time and how to take advantage of it.

First Line ▬ ▬

Take great care. To do so means to pay attention to all related events and not to act too forcefully. The I Ching often counsels us to notice when others are open to us, which is a time to move forward with them; when the person is not open to us is when we should do or say nothing. Have you noticed that on some days teachers are open to you and on other days they are not? Pay attention and consider this swing in others' receptivity when talking with them. Circumstances and people are always changing. So it is the wise person, even during extraordinary times, who pays attention to such changes in people and events.

Second Line ▬▬▬

Your relationship with another is beginning to heal and be restored. However, caution is still important. If you rush into things you may exceed the potential of the situation and miss the opportunity.

Third Line ▬▬▬

It is a perilous time, so you must be extra careful. Often when a time is full of potential it is also full of risk. Your choices now will have a lasting impact, so choose carefully. Do not force anything; take your time.

Fourth Line ━━━━━━━

You have captured people's affection because of your maturity and approachability. You are not arrogant, even though you are enjoying a time of great potential and opportunity. It is your reliance and awareness on spiritual principles and your Higher Power that has brought on much of this abundance.

Fifth Line ━━━ ━━━

Repairing a damaged relationship depends on your communicating honestly and openly about the earlier misunderstanding. You are considering renewing a relationship by ignoring what it was that caused problems between you. Therefore, the same problem will arise if you do not discuss it openly.

Sixth Line ━━━ ━━━

To take advantage of a time full of potential without any caution will lead to danger. For example, let's say you had admired someone from afar for quite some time. Now this person is showing an interest in you! People you trust have warned you about this person, however. Jumping into this relationship without facing the concerns head-on will likely result in you getting hurt. We are meant to reject some potential situations. Another opportunity will come and take its place. Go into your opportunities slowly and with your eyes open and good will result.

Consider

Find a story of someone, or interview someone, who has made great achievements in his or her life. Choose someone who holds similar interests as your own. How did this person handle success? When under the pressure of extraordinary times and potential, what did this person do? Or, how do you imagine this person handles his or her extraordinary times?

Water above

Water below

29

Living the Tao

All the fish needs
Is to get lost in the water.
All man needs is to get lost
In Tao.

—Chuang-tzu, fourth-century B.C. Chinese mystic and philosopher

The Tao (pronounced "dow") is the ideal; it is the part of us that is free of doubt, strong in our principles, that which is universal. It is the source of life, of change; it is the here and now, and it is our destiny. There is no Western word that holds the same meaning. The Tao is the "Unifying Principle," that which brings everything together and gets us through the most difficult of times. It brings everything together into a meaningful way, bringing hope out of despair, harmony out of chaos, joy out of suffering. The Tao is the connecting (invisible) thread that unifies all things, even those things that appear unrelated.

Receiving this hexagram means that it is time to identify the Tao in your life.

Everything you do and experience can be used for higher purposes by the Tao. You are in a dark time, because something seems to have failed. In this situation, as always, solutions are available—you only need to take the time to find them. The way out of the darkness is to connect with the Tao, to recognize the light in the darkness, to connect with your spiritual source. Your spiritual source, whatever form it takes for you, is the vehicle of the Tao. Spirit is completely in the Tao. And the Tao knows how to make everything work out for the best for all concerned. This is its very nature, to bring things to a favorable conclusion.

Where do you find the Tao? The image associated with this hexagram is an abyss. You may be in the darkness of the abyss, which could be understood as being consumed by the Tao. Using your intuition, meditating and listening for the Tao, and claiming your inner independence will all clear a way through the darkness. You do not have to *do* much, simply look and listen *within,* and the Tao will reveal itself to you.

First Line ━━ ━━

If you give in to worry and doubt, they can grow into a mind-set and cause great and unnecessary suffering. Worrying is fruitless—it doesn't prevent something from happening or repair any harm already done. Practice acceptance of the situation and open to the Tao by attending to other needs.

Second Line ━━━━

This is not the time to take big steps. Instead, slow down and listen for the Tao through meditation, quiet reflection, and going for nature walks. Be content with small steps and small progress.

Third Line ━━ ━━

Do not take any action. Get out of the situation by focusing on patient acceptance, opening up to the Tao, and involving yourself with other important matters—whatever is causing darkness is not the only thing happening in your life.

Fourth Line ━━ ━━

Your Higher Power knows that you are confused, doubtful, and worried. It comes to your aid to offer you help. This help will come as a breakthrough in your understanding of the situation. This means that you have succeeded at perceiving the principle of the Tao.

Fifth Line ━━━━

The darkness will fall away and give way to light as long as you don't get caught up in trying to resolve it all on your own. "All on your own" means without the help of your spiritual source, excluding the Tao and forgetting the principles of the I Ching.

Sixth Line ━━ ━━

If you remain stuck on how things "should" be or appear, this will only make matters worse for you. Remember the Tao is in every situation, no matter how bleak. If you trust your heart and the help of your Higher Power, things will work out. With a true and open heart, it is possible to make it through any situation because you are in contact with the principle of the Tao. And the Tao brings all things together in a good way.

Consider

In the Mahayana practice of Buddhism there is a practice called Lojong, "mind training." This practice offers fifty-nine pithy phrases that help us live a compassionate and fulfilled life. In essence it helps us connect regularly with the underlying principle of the Tao, that which exists in all things. It does this by training our minds (and hearts) to open and soften to ourselves and to our life's circumstances. For more information, see Pema Chödrön's *Start Where You Are: A Guide to Compassionate Living* (Shambhala, Boston: 1994).

The thirteenth slogan is "Be grateful to everyone." This means that within every situation, no matter how dark, the Tao is there. Because this is so, because the Tao is present in everything, we can easily be grateful even for those who cause us pain and even to those who disrupt our lives! Because they bother us, we are pushed to search for the Tao. If they didn't disrupt our lives, we might forget to work on our spiritual principles. So, this time of darkness with all its discomfort helps us search for the Tao. Therefore, we can "be grateful to everyone."

Practice this slogan for a week. Write it out on Post-its and put them in your car, on your bathroom mirror, on your refrigerator. Practice this slogan and notice how often you come in contact with the Tao.

Fire above

Fire below

30

Flaming Rainbow

Within you is a flame. It's inextinguishable. It never dies. It is searching for a place to alight and set fire. Listen to this internal heat, and go in search of that which is in search of you.
—Flaming Rainbow Woman, Spiritual Warrior

Fire can burn only when it receives its sustenance from wood; it must cling to something in order to burn. You might say that fire is always in search of its source of heat. And this source is in turn in search of its fire. Everything that you want to express, be it wealth, love, friendship, purpose, or fun, also wants to express itself within you. Money is nothing but paper until it connects up with someone to use it. Love is something that is given and received (even in the case of self-love). Friendship takes more than one person. To have a purpose expressed takes necessity and

a person to embody it. Every dream and intent you hold inside yourself is also looking for its way to you. That which you are searching for is also searching for you.

Nothing can kill that internal flame within you, but it can, through abuse, become a very small ember. So it is vital that this internal flame cling to a spiritual source and spiritual principles. As you practice the principles offered to you through the I Ching, the flame will intensify. This hexagram is about clinging to spiritual principles in order to sustain an internal flame. Your fire can burn only when it has something substantial to cling to. Clinging to doubt and fear offers little or no true power. So, cling to higher principles such as hope, love, and creativity and the flame will endure and burn strong.

First Line ━━━━

Don't let your own doubts or the doubts of others infect your dreams. Approach your dream with patience and openness.

Second Line ━━ ━━

The principle to cling to here is balance and moderation. How can you bring balance into the situation?

Third Line ━━━━

Try not to rush yourself through these teenage years. Rushing to do everything and as much as possible may quickly burn you out! Doing too much doesn't fan your internal flame. Putting too much wood on a flame only puts it out, leaving only an ember and some smoke. Slow down, choose wisely, and enjoy.

Fourth Line ━━━━

A principle to cling to throughout your teenage years is the power of positive thinking. If you are obsessing over worries and concerns, you will only attract more worries and concerns. Have you ever been around someone who complains a lot? Have you noticed how this person always has a lot *to* complain about? Cling to doubt and worries, and you will be doubtful and worried. Cling to patience and hope, and you will be patient and hopeful.

Fifth Line ▬ ▬

A real change of heart can take place in you or another if you cling to your Higher Power and spiritual principles.

Sixth Line ▬▬▬

Impatience and doubt are welling again, which means you are clinging to negative sources of power. Return to patience and acceptance, and in time things will work out. Have patience—things take as long as they take—and accept that which you are searching for is also searching for you.

Consider

Build a sacred fire. Build a fire in a pit where you can observe how the flames are dependent on the wood to exist. Think about how what you are searching for is also searching for you. Right now, that person, that dream, is also in search of you to set itself ablaze. Without you it will not fully exist. Without wood to burn, there would be no flame. Without earth to cling to, there would be no trees. Ponder the principles you need to cling to in order to sustain and build your flame. Contemplate how clinging to your Higher Power gives you energy. Most certainly, when we go in search of our spiritual nourishment, it is also in search of us—it wants to express itself through us! This means that we only have to do half of the work—that which we are searching for is doing its part to get to us.

As the flames rise and fall, showing off their rainbow of colors, think about these things.

A luminous thing giving out light must have within itself something that
perseveres; otherwise it will in time burn itself out. Everything that
gives light is dependent on something to which it clings,
in order that it may continue to shine.
**—Richard Wilhelm and Cary F. Baynes,
from *The I Ching or Book of Changes*, hexagram 30**

Lake above

Mountain below

31

Attraction

I find that what I put out there is what I get back. I put out good things about others, and good people come into my life. It can be a scary idea, because we have to watch what we put out there. But it's awesome when it works in a good way.
—Coleman Peters, age 18

Have you ever heard it said that if you sit in the barber's chair long enough, you are bound to get a hair cut? Some anonymous speaker at a twelve-step program said this. For him it was about admitting that if we frequent bars long enough we are sure to drink! The same is true for almost everything: our thoughts, the attitudes we cling to, and the dreams we hope for all eventually manifest into something real. When we focus on higher principles and hang out with those who share these principles, we find ourselves surrounded by goodwill. On the other hand, when we gossip about others or put others down, we attract others who do the same. Even if we just hang out long enough with those who gossip about others, we will find ourselves doing the same. Receiving this hexagram can indicate that an influence is about to take place. This may be the influence of another, of your spiritual source or a pleasant or unpleasant event. Prepare yourself for an influence by reflecting on what you are attracted to and what is attracted to you. What do you tend to attract into your life?

To attract certain people and experiences into our lives, we need to develop the qualities in ourselves we want in others. Let goodness dominate your thoughts and actions. Be mindful of the places you frequent and the people you associate with. Do you keep putting yourself in favorable or unfavorable places? Receiving this hexagram means that whatever it is that is coming into your life now (good or bad) has been attracted to you by your attitude and choices.

First Line ▬ ▬

You have your foot in the door, so to speak. You have attracted an opportunity where you can have a positive influence if you practice a generous and receptive attitude.

Second Line ▬ ▬

Do not be attracted to someone or something by appearances alone. Give yourself time to see and understand more about the situation or person. Appearances are only the "packaging" and can be misleading.

Third Line ▬▬▬

Be careful not to be seduced into making a quick decision. Those who truly care about your well-being will not try to rush you into a decision. Take your time and pay attention to detail. Be careful of flattery; this is usually only a technique of seduction, not someone's genuine feelings.

Fourth Line ▬▬▬

Let go of your expectations of how others should behave. If you get too caught up in trying to attract another person to you, what is meant to happen gets lost. You can lose clarity and good judgment if you try to push a relationship. Let relationships evolve naturally.

Fifth Line ━━━

Don't chase others. Instead, allow for a natural and spontaneous attraction to occur. If it is meant to be, it will be.

Sixth Line ━━ ━━

Talk less and act more. Show others who you are by your actions, not your words. And trust the love and wisdom of your Higher Power who is helping you with this situation.

Consider

Take some time to inventory the places you frequent as well as who you are choosing as friends and why. What behaviors and attitudes do these places and people encourage? What qualities do these people and places bring out in you?

Thunder above

Wind below

32

The Web of Life

Think about wheels any time you like.
Any little wheel you see is worth looking at.
The sun is a wheel, the moon is a wheel.
Many a night star is a wheel.

And in your head, in many little places behind
*   Your blinking wonderful eyes, you can find,*
*   If you try, ten thousand wheels within wheels.*
—Carl Sandburg, poet, "Think about Wheels," from
Poems for Children Nowhere Near Old Enough to Vote

This hexagram is about things that endure. We can get through all the changes in life (and during our teen years change is constant) when we bring forth enduring qualities such as love, compassion, tolerance, and friendship. No matter what changes take place in our lives, we are to remain true to that which endures.

All that is good and strong endures change. Change is at hand all the time during our teen years. All the more reason to nurture those qualities that will last, such as compassion, patience, love, acceptance, inner independence, and tolerance. We then bring these qualities into our relationships. If you are inquiring about a friendship or romantic relationship, know that it will last if you both weave in these qualities.

It can be helpful during these years of transition to remember that we are all part of the web of life, and the moment each of us is born a place is made for us. You might say we were born with a blueprint that includes a place and purpose for our lives. Receiving this hexagram is a reminder to be cognizant of your part in this great web, which endures lifetime after lifetime. Even death is part of the web of life—the *life-death-life cycle*. When we die we are changing once again into something new, but the soul endures. If we could remember back to the time we spent in the womb, we would recall the contractions that occurred before we were pushed out through the birth canal into the world and into the arms of our mother. In death, we will feel the same contractions once again, as we are pushed out of this body, down a birth canal, and into the arms of the Great Mother.

If you've experienced a recent loss, you have received this hexagram as a reminder that the love you had with this person endures.

First Line ▬ ▬

Do not expect too much too soon. Most things of quality take a long time to develop. Do not expect a relationship to start out intimate and committed. Mature love and lasting friendships take time to develop.

Second Line ▬▬▬

Once you realize that you've made a mistake, admit it and move on. No need to rehash the mistake in your mind. No need for regret. It is enough that you have the insight and strength to conclude your mistake and move on.

Third Line ▬▬▬

Anytime you compare yourself to your peers to measure your own progress and worth, you lose sight of the spiritual truths that sustain us. Comparing yourself to others arouses judgment, doubt, and anxiety. Let others go their way and you go yours, allowing for differences.

Fourth Line ▬▬▬

Concentrate on your attitude and approach to life and less on the outcome. Outcomes are important, but it is the journey that really counts.

Fifth Line ▬▬ ▬▬

Let others go their own way and discover their own truths. It is not your duty to direct or control others. If you are meant to be together in friendship or in love, you will meet again.

Sixth Line ▬▬ ▬▬

Throughout our lives we need to let go and let the circle of life do its dance around us and with us. We shouldn't always be doing, doing, doing. Receiving this line means that it is time to relax into the circle of life and not push anything forward. Let what comes to you come in its own way and time.

Consider

Confucius says,

Sun and Moon rely on the Tao of Heaven;
Thus can their shining be long lasting.
The four seasons change and transform;
Thus can their production of beings long endure.
The holy sage remains long lasting in his way of life;
Then all beings under Heaven are transformed to completion.
Contemplate the Tao of Long Lasting,*
To see the Nature of Heaven and Earth and of all beings.

**—Taoist Master Alfred Huang,
from *The Complete I Ching*, hexagram 32**

———————
*Contemplate the Tao of the Web of Life

Heaven above

Mountain below

33

Backing Off

When you are feeling depreciated, angry, or drained, it is a sign that other people are not open to your energy.
—Sanaya Roman, author of *Creating Money: Keys to Abundance*, from *The Artist's Way*

Sometimes we come into contact with forces and people who are not good for us. The way in which people undermine you may be subtle or it may be obvious. They may be insisting that you join them in some negative and harmful behavior. Or, they may want you to share in a belief that is highly toxic. They simply may be trying to engage you in a fight. Because such dark forces are at play now, it is time for you to back off. Anyone who insists that you participate in something harmful does not care about you. But your present situation cannot be entirely avoided. The best you can do is back off quietly and wait for the time to either approach this person or end the relationship.

Backing Off

The image of this hexagram is of mountain under heaven; it is by keeping our distance with dignity that we will succeed. A mountain stands apart in dignity. Backing off is not the same as giving up or giving in. It is not the same as running away from commitments. A strong person knows when and how to back off from potentially harmful times. To back off in dignity now will benefit you in the end.

Receiving this hexagram may mean that you and a friend are in a conflict. At this time your friend is not ready to communicate or resolve the issue. Do not try to force your friend to work things out. Forcing yourself on your friend will only increase the discourse. Back off from the fight and give both of you space and time to think things through. Take advantage of this time apart to further understand the other person's ideas and way of thinking. This does not mean that you have to agree, but you should strive for understanding. Every relationship has limits; perhaps you have come up against one at this time. It may also be that this relationship needs to end. Time will tell.

First Line ━━ ━━

You are still caught up in a situation from which you need to back off. Are you making a compromise about something you know isn't correct for you? Or, are you hooked by feelings of anger, fear, or anxiety and need to prove something? You must back off and stop thinking and worrying about the situation.

Second Line ━━ ━━

Of course you want what is fair, and you want to be heard! But if you feel that you have to force your opinions on others, it is likely that they are not open to what you have to say anyway. You can want fairness, but don't expect it from this situation. You will win the help of your Higher Power when you succeed at backing off and not trying to force your point on others.

Third Line ━━━━

Even though you have backed off from the situation, you are mentally engaged in conflict. Let the situation work itself out while you go about getting other things done (there is more to your life than this situation or relationship). It may be helpful for you to journal why you are so obsessed about this situation.

Fourth Line ━━━

It is a great challenge for all of us to disengage from conflict, especially if it isn't resolved. You have successfully backed away from a conflict, and this is a great accomplishment. Once you removed yourself from the situation, the other person no longer had anyone to fight with and gave up. In a sense, you gave him or her nothing to push against.

Fifth Line ━━━

Continue to remain disengaged from the negative forces. Be strong and kind in your withdrawal. The others may try to get you involved in the fight again, because they don't want to fight with themselves. Do not let yourself be hooked again. Remain detached and patient. Others can hook us back into negative forces when we get impatient for *something* to happen. When you remain tolerant and firm in your retreat, you will not be seduced back into conflict. This is backing off with dignity.

Sixth Line ━━━

When we come to understand the value of backing away from negative forces, better opportunities open up for us. This is a great skill to have, and you are free now to do your own thing because you are no longer struggling with the negative force.

Consider

What would help you to back off from a situation so you can gain some perspective? You may want to go on a short trip, focus on other things, visit a grandparent, meditate, listen to a particular song, or go to a movie. Give yourself the means to back off with dignity from the situation.

Thunder above

Heaven below

34

Authentic Power

*It takes courage to grow up and turn out to be who
you really are.*
—**e.e. cummings, poet and painter**

You have developed authentic power by applying spiritual principles and relying on the help of your Higher Power. Opportunities are emerging for you, and you are feeling *empowered*. You are learning how to make things happen in your favor by applying spiritual principles. You are tapping in to the Tao (see hexagram 29), and this fills you with strength and energy.

It is important to remember that this power endures when we continue to apply good spiritual principles. The I Ching warns us not to exploit this power by becoming arrogant, judgmental, or manipulative. There is a tendency to dismiss others when we are feeling powerful. However, *authentic* power serves everyone we come in contact with. The more power we obtain, the more responsibility we have to treat others well. For example, be patient with others who have not obtained their power yet. The I Ching counsels us to be mindful of what we say to others, as this influences both parties.

During your teen years you are likely to encounter these surges of personal power many, many times. Such times can ignite restlessness. Therefore, learning to harness this power will generate more opportunities for you. Consider how you want to cultivate this power, and it will support you and others along the way.

First Line ━━━

Can you have your power without trying to get others to acknowledge it? If you try too hard to prove yourself, this may lead to embarrassment. Return to a more balanced state of mind and events will work out.

Second Line ━━━

To avoid abusing your power, remain strong and discreet. You can benefit and use all your power without hurting others. You will be recognized for your moral strength, but not because of any insistence on your part.

Third Line ━━━

You are butting your head against a brick wall, and only your head is damaged. A well-developed and truly powerful person uses his or her abilities skillfully, not by demanding recognition from others. It takes great insight and skill to know when to act and when not to act.

Fourth Line ━━━

You are about to compromise your power by doubting yourself just because you made a mistake. Use your authentic power to transform the mistake into a blessing. You can do this.

Fifth Line ━━ ━━

You don't need to be defensive to protect yourself. Putting up walls only takes energy away from your power. A lot of energy goes into keeping the wall up and defending yourself. Lighten up, and trust that things can and will work out. Let your guard down, and no harm will come to you.

Sixth Line ▬▬ ▬▬

Misuse of your power has brought on more difficulty rather than helping you out. If you recognize this in time and correct yourself, everything will work out.

大
壯

Consider

Discover your power animal (totem). Discovering what your animal totem is helps you develop this power in yourself. This tradition is borrowed from Native American and Japanese shamanic practices. Either by seeking the help of a shamanic healer, recalling your dreams, or going on a medicine walk, you can discover your power animal.

A medicine walk is a walk in a natural setting (forest, prairie, park) where you can go in search of an encounter with an animal. The "medicine" of this walk is the encounters you have with wildlife and the meaning you attach to these encounters. Give yourself at least one hour (two to four is better). Find a place where you are likely to encounter something wild, be it an insect, bird, coyote, deer, kangaroo, even a fish swimming near the shore. Choose something that symbolizes a threshold that you pass through as you leave the everyday world and enter the sacred world of the Spirit. This can be a tree you walk under, a branch you walk over, or an arbor you pass through.

When you go on your walk, walk slowly and quietly. You may want to sit down in one spot for some time to see what approaches you. Then simply notice what animal appears on your walk. It may be a track or dwelling of an animal or even the droppings of an animal (so watch where you step!). Some have said that they encountered the sound of an animal. Your dreams may also bring to you your power animals. Ask before going to sleep to be visited by your power animal and see what shows up.

There are many CDs and tapes that can guide you through a meditative journey where you go in search of your power animal. The titles of these materials will indicate that they are meant for shamanic journeying. Many new age bookstores have such CDs. Information about shamanic journeying and finding your power animal can be found in Michael Harner's book *The Way of the Shaman* (San Francisco: Harper San Francisco, 1990) and Kenneth Meadows's book *Earth Medicine: Revealing Hidden Teachings of the Native American Medicine Wheel* (Rockport, Mass.: Element, 1996). Or, to find a shamanic healer in your area, contact the Foundation for Shamanic Studies, P.O. Box 1939, Mill Valley, CA 94942; tel: 415-380-8282.

You can also consider what animal totem (power animal) is yours by considering the following questions:

1. What animal, insect, or bird has tended to get your attention? We are attracted to those animals that express our powers and have something to teach us.

2. What animal have you most frequently encountered in nature or in your dreams?

3. What animal do you hope your power animal will be? Every animal holds its own type of authentic power.

4. What animal do you fear? The animals we fear also have something to teach us about their power, and our own power.

An aminal totem mirrors aspects of our *own* nature . . .
—**Kenneth Meadows,**
author of *Earth Medicine: Revealing Hidden Teachings*
of the *Native American Medicine Wheel*

Fire above

Earth below

35

Improvement

There is a crack in everything, and that is how the
light gets in.
—Leonard Cohen, poet and singer

The image of this hexagram is of the sun rising above the earth. Everything the sun touches is encouraged to grow, to improve, to mature. The sun also "eats up" the darkness in order to create the light. The light of the sun can shine through the smallest of openings, lighting up the entire space. We all have cracks in our thought processes; we all hold dark and negative energies inside. Bringing the light energy to these dark places can transform them. We can bring the sun to negative emotions such as hatred and jealousy and convert them into love and compassion.

This is a time of improvement and light for you. The improvement is coming easily and naturally. The sun is rising and shining on your life right now. The more light you let in, the greater the improvement. Let the light shine on every aspect of your life. Brighten your life with a positive and healthy attitude.

Receiving this hexagram can mean that a friend and you are a good match. You complement one another. You have the potential for a creative, safe, and enduring relationship.

First line ━━ ━━

Even though you are acting correctly, you lack confidence in yourself. Keep doing what you know to be correct, and feelings of confidence will follow in time.

Second Line ━━ ━━

No relationship is worth compromising yourself for by going against what you feel is right. As the French philosopher André Gide said, "It is better to be hated for who we are than loved for who we are not." Be true to yourself first, and you will attract supportive and loving people.

Third Line ━━ ━━

Others will come to support you and benefit from your improvement when you live by your inner truth.

Fourth Line ━━━━

When times and relationships are improving, we have to be careful not to become careless and greedy, like the captain of the *Titanic* who got overzealous and lost sight of the limits of the ship. His carelessness harmed everyone on that ship. We all need to be careful when we are sitting in a position of power and improvement, so as not to lose sight of our limits. Doing so will keep you safe from danger.

Fifth Line ━━ ━━

Sometimes we lose sight of the Big Picture in our teen years and get too caught up in each disappointment and improvement as if it is the last. Try to maintain a sense of *journey* and that this improvement is just one passage of the journey; there are countless more.

Sixth Line ━━━━

Being hard or thoughtless with others only backfires on you. Aggression is justified only against our own negative elements. Prevent yourself from being hard on others and the situation will continue to improve.

晋

Consider

Get up in time to watch the sun rise. If possible go outside while it is still dark, and wait on the rising sun. Then watch and notice when the sun touches everything with its light—including you.

How
Did the rose
Ever open its heart

And give to this world
All its
Beauty?

It felt the encouragement of light
Against its
Being,
Otherwise,
We all remain

Too
Frightened.

**—Hafiz, Sufi master,
from *The Gift: Poems by Hafiz***

明夷

36

A Time of Darkness

*Flowers and even fruit are only the beginning. In
the seed lies the life and the future.*
—Marion Zimmer Bradley, poet and author of *The Mists of Avalon*

This is a time to keep to yourself, because darkness and difficulty surround you.
The image is of the setting sun. The darkness you experience is a result of outside
circumstances that surround you. Just as a sun rises (hexagram 35), it also must
set. Since the darkness is just beginning, progress will be slow, but there will, in
time, be improvement. The situation seems hopeless, and because of this you are
discouraged. You are afraid that you will never find a way out of the darkness.
Things do have a way of working out in time, so concentrate on keeping your faith
and rely on the help of your spiritual source to get you through this time.

The goodness inside of you can help you get through this time as well. Since the

darkness seems unbearably long, focus on your inner strengths. Just as times of light and improvement are part of life (hexagram 35), times of great darkness and hardship are inevitable as well. The key to a successful transition is to learn to persevere through these dark times without giving up on yourself or your Higher Power.

Accept your situation as an inevitable dark time, and in time the light will break through the darkness. Receiving this hexagram may mean that others are keeping you in the dark about something. There is not much you can do but trust your intuition and wait out the dark time. With an accepting attitude things will work out. The sun will rise again.

First Line ——————

Because you are afraid that nothing will work out for you, you are tempted to give up on higher principles. To act out of despair will only bring more darkness. Hold on to patience, and trust in your Higher Power. In the dark the creative force is at work—remember this.

Second Line —— ——

Sometimes the best thing that you can do when you are hurting is to let go of the situation and help someone else. By offering help to someone else now you will experience some relief.

Third Line ——————

You have reached an understanding about the present hardship. However, this does not mean that an immediate solution is at hand. Hang in there, and hold on to your Inner Truth, and in time, the situation will improve.

Fourth Line —— ——

Once you recognize a negativity within yourself or the situation, do not hang on to it, but leave it behind and move on. Hanging on to negativity results in more darkness. (An example of such negativity is holding on to hopelessness and believing there is no end to the hardship.) Leaving the negative path behind brings improvement.

Fifth Line ▬ ▬

The hardship cannot be avoided now. Accept the situation while building your inner strength.

Sixth Line ▬ ▬

The darkness is peaking. You probably feel as if everything you tried to do failed to change the circumstances. The darkness cannot harm you if you remain strong and independent. Do not fall into negativity and hopelessness, and good will soon prevail.

Consider

Find a quiet place in nature and watch the sun set. Notice the light as it is eaten up by the darkness and the colors of the setting sun. Think on how one day has come to an end again and soon everything around you will be waiting and resting in the darkness. Consider how being in the dark is just another process of life.

Wind above

Fire below

家

人

37

The Family
and the Gang

First
The fish needs to say,

"Something ain't right about this
Camel ride—

And I'm
Feeling so damn

Thirsty."
—Hafiz, Sufi master, from *The Gift: Poems by Hafiz*

This hexagram is about creating and living in healthy families and communities. What is the condition of your family environment? As teenagers we cannot always get out of a negative environment, but we can do our best to take care of ourselves within this environment. As we improve ourselves we offer a positive influence to our environment. And regardless of our family situations, we can choose our own paths.

In healthy families we see reflected qualities such as respect, honesty, faithfulness, safety, and an affinity for one another. When we truly love another person, we are instinctively generous, kind, and accepting of each other. You cannot make someone else acquire these qualities, but you can nurture them in yourself. You will then draw to you others who cultivate the same higher principles. Depending on how many qualities your family possesses, or lacks, will determine what challenges you face in your relationships.

An ancient proverb explains that if you want to heal the world, you must first heal the community; if you want to heal the community, you must first heal the family; if you want to heal the family, you must first heal yourself. In healing yourself, all those around you benefit. Receiving this hexagram reminds you to ask yourself what it is that you bring into your relationships. What has your family taught you about love and commitment?

In some cases "the family" can refer to a group, clan, clique, or gang to which one belongs. In order to create a healthy group, everyone needs to cling to the principles that make up a healthy family. If a group is promoting cruel, unsafe, or incorrect principles, it is not a good place to remain. If it is difficult to leave the group, seek help from the outside.

First Line ━━━

There are issues in your close relationships that need to be dealt with. Solve these first, applying the principles you have learned in consulting the I Ching. Begin at the beginning, with yourself and your close relationships.

Second Line ━━ ━━

Be careful not to get caught up in what others should or shouldn't be doing. In relationships it is too easy for us to be aware of how we think the *other* needs to change, losing sight of our own issues. This line is also about you giving too much attention to the past or to planning the future. Return your attention to the present situation.

Third Line ———

Learn to be gentle with yourself, and this will make it easier to be gentle with others. When you are gentle with yourself and others, you avoid being too extreme in your feelings and reactions to changing situations.

Fourth Line — —

Feeling afraid and discouraged about your future makes you want to give up and isolate yourself from others. We all need the support of family or a healthy community to get us through discouraging times. Reach out to those who love you, and let them offer you encouragement.

Fifth Line ———

People who create fear in you or others are best avoided. Ongoing fear creates a loss of inner power and peace. Love, on the other hand, opens doors. Do what you can to open doors.

Sixth Line ———

Your relationships are good and reflect your efforts to become a person who possesses great qualities. Your feet are firmly on the spiritual path, and you are surrounded with a loving community.

Consider

What makes a cult? Learn to identify a cult or controlling individual. Educate yourself on what constitutes emotional or psychological abuse so that these relationships can be avoided. Here are a few characteristics of cults and possessive relationships:

- You are not given permission to disagree.
- Someone else wants to do the thinking and decision making for you.
- You feel undermined.
- The more time you spend with this group or person, the more you become isolated from friends and family.

Fire above

Lake below

38

Misunderstandings

Boundless wind and moon—the eye within eyes,
Inexhaustible heaven and earth—the light beyond
    light,
The willow dark, the flower bright—ten thousand
    houses;
Knock at any door—there's one who will respond.
—Rumi, Sufi poet

A misunderstanding has occurred. This misunderstanding can be between you and another; it may mean that you misunderstand life's meaning for you, or you misunderstand the counsel of the I Ching. The misunderstanding is great, and it would be wise to seek the help of a qualified counselor or spiritual teacher who can help you come to an understanding within yourself. If you have a mentor, seek his or her help at this time.

Receiving this hexagram may mean that you are misunderstanding someone or someone is misunderstanding you. Do not try to force a fast reconciliation. Instead, let the other person go his or her own way while you acquire insight into the misunderstanding. Once you gain some understanding of the situation and are open to listen to the other person, there will be an opportunity to get together.

You may be misunderstanding a basic truth while trying to rationalize a negative habit. For example, when we want to continue the harmful habit of abusing drugs, we make up reasons why it really isn't so harmful. What can you do to gain some perspective? With your concern?

First Line ━━━━

Even though the misunderstanding is big, there is an opportunity for unity. Without trying to force anything, simply remain open to the other person or to your own inner truth.

Second Line ━━━━

A small breakthrough in the misunderstanding is accomplished by your trusting in the good. Such openness always leads to understanding. It is as if you were sitting in a small closed room and with your trust opened the doors and windows only to realized that the room is quite a bit larger than you had thought. With this spaciousness, you now have room for more possibilities.

Third Line ━━ ━━

Everything seems to be going against you. Handle this difficulty as a test and respond in a balanced way by not overreacting. Accept the situation patiently, and good will result.

Fourth Line ━━━━

Seek the help of friends and family to help clarify the misunderstanding.

Fifth Line ━━ ━━

When you are tangled up in a misunderstanding, it is difficult to see what possibilities there are for you. Try to see beyond the surface of things and gain a larger perspective. If you succeed at doing this, a positive outcome will result.

Sixth Line ━━━

No one is out to get you. Stop being stressed, and relax in the knowledge that things have a way of working out.

Consider

Once there was a woman who was sent to jail. She had been in jail for quite some time and had forgotten what she did to get there. There was a small window in this jail that allowed the sun to shine into the cell for one hour at noon each day. The woman would wait for the sun to come to the window and would pull herself up out of the darkness, holding her face in the small opening. She would hang from the window until the sun passed. Then she would drop down into the dark and sit. At some point someone would come in and place a dish of food in the dark, and she would eat. All day and night she would be in the dark, sitting and sleeping in the corner, until the sun came to the window again. Each day she would use all her strength to pull herself up and keep her face in the sun. This went on for her entire lifetime. What she did not notice was that at any time she could leave, for there was no lock on the door.

Are you misunderstanding a situation because you are in the dark? Are you focused on only one possibility, missing the real opportunity in the situation? If the woman had simply moved herself around, or tried the door, or looked around the room when the sun arrived, she might have seen that there was no lock on the door and that she was free to go at any time. She could have talked to the person bringing her food and perhaps discovered that she could leave when she was ready.

Her jailers needed no lock to keep her prisoner.

> The truth is always there,
> usually right under our noses. Just
> don't let the size of your nose
> block your view.
>
> **—Jere Truer, poet**

```
▬▬▬▬    ▬▬▬▬
▬▬▬▬▬▬▬▬▬▬▬▬
▬▬▬▬    ▬▬▬▬
▬▬▬▬▬▬▬▬▬▬▬▬
▬▬▬▬    ▬▬▬▬
▬▬▬▬    ▬▬▬▬
```

Water above

Mountain below

39

Between a Rock and a Hard Place

A hungry dog bites a dry bone.
—Soiku Shigematsu, translator of *A Zen Forest*

You are besieged with feelings of hopelessness, doubt, low self-esteem, and fear. Being in such a spot makes it impossible to move. The only way to release yourself from these feelings is to challenge them and gain a new perspective. Unlike the time of darkness described in hexagram 36, this hexagram refers to a time of negative thoughts. When our thoughts are so heavy and gloomy, we are unable to make any progress.

We prevent our own peace of mind when we focus on the negative qualities in ourselves and others. There is a belief in the Mahayana Buddhist practice that if you think about love for yourself and others, you can't simultaneously think angry thoughts. It is important to begin with ourselves—bring love to all that you dislike about yourself and the love for others will come. We tend to feel toward others what we really feel about ourselves. Work on appreciating yourself, and all your qualities, and you will develop a friendship with yourself and others.

First Line ▬▬ ▬▬

It is time to learn from the present difficulty. This can happen by seeking the help of someone whose opinion you trust and by stepping back to gain a wider perspective of the situation. You will remain consumed by negative thoughts if you don't do something to acquire perspective. Getting unstuck becomes easy when you step back.

Second Line ▬▬ ▬▬

You are not the cause of the present difficulty. The trouble, however, provides an opportunity for you to develop inner strength. Instead of thinking negative thoughts about yourself, use this time to build yourself up. You have a tendency to take on hard and negative thoughts and then dwell on them. When we are stuck in such a hard place, we tend to judge others harshly as well. Only an open mind can see the way out of difficulty.

Third Line ▬▬▬

Good will come if you don't act impulsively. We act this way to try to get ourselves out of an uncomfortable spot, but it only worsens the situation. Do not tell others what to do; let them go their own way. Work on steering yourself away from negative thinking.

Fourth Line ▬▬ ▬▬

Through meditation and times of stillness you gain the strength necessary to move ahead. The correct action will be shown to you at the right time.

Fifth Line ▬▬▬

You begin to feel some release from being stuck in negativity. Focusing on correcting your negative thoughts is what is helping you in this situation. Furthermore, the Higher Power is coming to your aid.

Sixth Line —— ——

You are capable of helping yourself and helping others as well. This occurs when you are committed to higher principles and rely on the help of your spiritual source.

Consider

Hold on to a positive thought about yourself and notice that you cannot hold on to a negative at the same time. If the negative thought comes back, return your thoughts to something positive. This can be a one-time practice or a form of meditation. To meditate on positive thoughts, sit in a meditative posture with your back straight and not reclining against anything. Have your feet on the floor if you are sitting on a chair. Be comfortable, yet upright and alert. Begin with this breath meditation: Find your breath, and for a moment relax into the breath. Simply imagine your breath moving through your body. Notice the physical sensation of breath. Then focus your awareness on one positive thought, such as "I am filled with loving thoughts." Continue to repeat this thought. Feel yourself fill with loving thoughts. Notice that you cannot hold on to the negative thinking and this positive thought at the same time. Sit for a few minutes, basking in these good and loving thoughts.

The highest wisdom is loving-kindness.

—The Talmud

Thunder above

Water below

40

Freedom

Be the cause of your life, rather than the effect. Know that in every situation you have what it takes to be free of negativity and harm. Your freedom comes when you really get that what you think about circumstances determines your experience.
—Flaming Rainbow Woman, Spiritual Warrior

You are soon to be freed from some difficulty, stress, or danger. True freedom comes from a change in attitude first, then the needed changes in environment can take place. This is why the I Ching and many other spiritual practices focus on purifying our thoughts. It is what we *think* about a situation that really determines how things will work out for us. Bad and good happen throughout our lifetimes—we can be free of riding the roller coaster of these circumstances when we learn to be the *cause* of our lives. To be the cause means that we live by the knowledge that how we respond to circumstances will determine the outcome. Things don't just happen to us—we are not entirely at the mercy of outside forces. Even though many times during our teen years and throughout our adult lives it can seem as though we have no power or freedom; we do. We always have the freedom to decide how to handle a given difficulty or opportunity.

The image that accompanies this hexagram is that of a thunderstorm with heavy rain that washes the dirt (difficulty) away. Once we obtain freedom, it is a good time to start over, begin fresh. Let the past be washed away. This could mean that there is someone we need to forgive (possibly ourselves). In order to be truly free, we need to continually let go of the past through the act of forgiveness.

The lines in this hexagram reflect specific problems in our attitudes that prevent us from experiencing freedom.

First Line ▬▬ ▬▬

You have gotten through a difficulty. Don't flaunt your success. An "I told you so" will backfire. Sometimes we want to antagonize those who have hurt us by showing them our successes. The moment you do this, your acquired freedom is lost.

Second Line ▬▬▬▬▬

Beware of wanting to make yourself look better than others. Instead, develop your character and good will follow you. When we are trying to prove ourselves to others, we can't experience freedom when our happiness is dependent on them recognizing us. Some days they will recognize us and some days they won't, depending on their moods and not our actions.

Third Line ▬▬ ▬▬

Once freed from trouble we may have the tendency to consider ourselves better than others. If you give in to such an attitude you will eventually be humiliated.

Fourth Line ▬▬▬▬▬

Don't respond to your problems as you have in the past. Take a look at how you usually handle such problems and see if you can come up with another way. (Hint: there are at least three other ways to respond to the problem successfully.)

Fifth Line — —

It is important to change your attitude, not other people. In fact, you have no control over others, but you can always change your attitude. Improve your attitude and you will be free from the problem.

Sixth Line — —

Sometimes the problem is the result of having the wrong perspective on things. Seek the help of your Higher Power and ask for a better perspective of the situation. You will receive a way to be free from the difficulty. Know that a change in viewpoint will be the greatest help.

Consider

Have you heard the story of how monkeys are caught in the Japanese rain forest? Hunters put out wooden cages with holes in one side large enough for the monkeys' hands. Inside they place the monkeys' favorite nuts. These nuts can be found throughout the jungle. Monkeys come along and see the nuts in the cages, put a hand in, and grab the nut. When they try to remove the nuts, they can't get the closed fist through the hole. To get free of the cage, all they have to do is let go of the nut and slide the hand out of the hole, but most monkeys won't let go of the nut, even though there are other nuts all over the jungle! All the hunter has to do is come up and cart the monkeys off to the zoo.

Is there something that you are holding on to that you need to release? Is someone "capturing" you with promises? Can you get a better perspective of the situation and see that there are other "nuts" available to you? Are you stubbornly holding on to an assumption?

Mountain above

Lake below

41

Disappointment

If you find a path with no obstacles, it probably
doesn't lead anywhere.
—Frank A. Clark, mathematician

Disappointments are common in life, but that doesn't make them any more pleasant. During our teen years disappointments often feel unbearable, because we already lack full control of our lives. Disappointments weigh heavily on the heart, so we need to heal from them as soon as possible.

You are experiencing a disappointment right now (or are about to) in the form of a limited opportunity, setback, rejection, unfulfilled expectation, or loss of some kind. First, be kind to yourself, which will make it a little easier to get through this time of disappointment. We can emerge from every disappointment stronger and wiser, depending on how we handle them. Second, don't blame others. Those who blame their disappointments on others or remain angry will generate more agony.

Be careful not to take the disappointment and turn it into a lasting attitude such as resentment, hopelessness, doubt in the power of good, or depression.

Even when others disappoint you (the best people have a way of doing this), be generous of heart in your handling of the situation. Those who love you will disappoint you, even though they don't mean to. If you are in a relationship with someone who continually disappoints you, perhaps it is time to reconsider this relationship.

First Line ━━━

Sometimes the best thing you can do when you are disappointed is to serve others. Help someone else in need and take your mind off your own disappointment.

Second Line ━━━

Do not put yourself down. Even though you have experienced a disappointment or setback, do not make it all about you. You don't have to explain yourself to those who are not open to hearing what you have to say.

Third Line ━━ ━━

When you stop putting yourself down, you make room in your mind for more positive and healthy thoughts. This line is also about making room in your heart and life for the help of your Higher Power. Do this by first asking for its help. Then, by quieting your mind (through meditation or contemplation) you can receive some insight into how to handle the disappointment. Another way that your Higher Power helps you is by providing you with a favorable circumstance. Watch for another opportunity opening up for you.

Fourth Line ━━ ━━

As a result of handling your disappointments well, and by cultivating a healthy attitude, the situation improves. This line counsels you not to compare yourself to others or focus on past disappointments.

Fifth Line ━━ ━━

Nothing and no one can prevent good from coming to you if you follow the good in yourself. (If your parents are alcoholic or abusive, please see the final box below.) Be true to yourself, and good fortune will find you.

Sixth Line ──────

Through self-discipline and seeking the help you need from others and your Higher Power, the situation improves dramatically. This is the time to share your abundance with others.

Consider

Help someone anonymously. Do something good for someone without asking for any recognition. Notice how it feels to help someone in this way. Notice how this also takes your mind away from your disappointments.

Also Consider

If you have alcoholic or abusive parents, chances are your life is full of disappointments that you have little or no control over. To save yourself from reaching a state of hopelessness and despair, reach out to others who can help. There are Ala-Teen groups available in every city. Or speak to your counselor at school. Don't try to handle your parents' addictions and the resulting disappointments alone. The sooner you reach out for help, the sooner you can begin building your life back up.

Wind above

Thunder below

42

Opportunity

The longer I live, the more beautiful life becomes.
—Frank Lloyd Wright, architect

Your life right now is full of opportunity and positive, powerful energy. You are meant to take advantage of this time of opportunity. This is not the time to kick back and relax but to make full use of this occasion. During this time of opportunity, even those things that appear as a disadvantage take on a more positive aspect and become an opportunity. Build on your opportunities. Each opportunity takes you closer and closer to your life's purpose. The I Ching counsels you to increase your blessings and build on this time of opportunity. Your rewards will then be multiplied.

There are two ways to help increase this occasion of opportunity. One is to be generous to others in thought, word, and deed. Be generous by being forgiving of other people's shortcomings. Seek out the best in everyone. Second, use this time to strengthen the good qualities in yourself.

Opportunity

First Line ━━━━

You are full of opportunity and are able to do a good deed for someone else. By being so generous you hold a sense of purpose in your heart and are able to accomplish even more.

Second Line ━━ ━━

If you focus on truth and goodness, nothing will stop you from achieving your dreams.

Third Line ━━ ━━

What appears as a difficulty holds great opportunity within it.

Fourth Line ━━ ━━

Take the middle road. Don't respond to the situation with extremes. A time of opportunity doesn't mean that you need to be off balance. Helping others can help keep you balanced.

Fifth Line ━━━━

True kindness and a desire to help others without having to be congratulated come spontaneously from the heart. It certainly is okay to accept praise, however. This attitude of wanting to help others just for the sake of helping others brings you happiness and the recognition you deserve.

Sixth Line ━━━━

It is important to help those around you when you have the abilities and resources to do so. Helping others in this way will lengthen your time of opportunity.

Consider

Once there was a man who died and found himself in a beautiful place surrounded by every conceivable comfort. A white-jacketed man came to him and said, "You may have anything you choose—any food, any pleasure, any kind of entertainment."

The man was delighted, and for days he sampled all the delicacies and experiences of which he had dreamed while alive. But one day he grew bored with these luxuries, and, calling the attendant to him, he said, "I'm tired of all this. I need something to do. What kind of work can you give me?"

The attendant sadly shook his head and replied, "I'm sorry, sir. That's the one thing we can't do for you. There is no work for you here."

The man answered, "That's a fine thing. I might as well be in hell."

The attendant said softly, "Where do you think you are?"

—Margaret Stevens, from *Stories of the Spirit, Stories of the Heart*

Lake above

Heaven below

43

Breakthrough

For behind all seen things lies something vaster;
everything is but a path, a portal, or a window
opening on something more than itself.
—Antoine de Saint-Exupéry, author of *The Little Prince*

What you have been waiting for is now at hand. A window has opened. Something that was difficult for you is now "breaking through" into a solution. Again, the I Ching counsels you to use this time wisely and to its greatest potential. The breakthrough can be in your understanding, where you come to have clarity about something you were recently upset and confused about. You may have felt disappointed or discouraged but now realize the potential behind the difficulty. This is a breakthrough in awareness and serves to positively influence everything. Breakthroughs are a special kind of opening that occur in our thinking, that allow more ideas and possibilities to occur to us. Many inventions are manifestations of such breakthroughs.

Receiving this hexagram can indicate that a breakthrough in a situation or relationship is occurring. In order to complete the breakthrough, be sure not to lose yourself in the intensity of it all. A breakthrough is a wonderful thing, and you are meant to take full advantage of it. If you become too intoxicated by the change, you will lose sight of what it is you need to do to fulfill the potential of the situation.

During a breakthrough, the I Ching suggests that we be an example for others. We can demonstrate to our families and peers the benefits of having lived by spiritual principles, such as those offered through the I Ching. Others will witness this in our behavior. Great and enduring success and happiness are available to those who make good use of this time of breakthrough.

First Line ━━━

You are stuck. Try not to get aggressive; instead, open yourself and try to figure out what is causing you to be so stuck. When we name things correctly (for example, "I am stuck in my feelings of anger"; "I am stuck in the belief that I am always at fault") we can respond accurately. Once you figure out what is causing you to be stuck, a breakthrough can occur.

Second Line ━━━

Remain aware of the possible dangers or problems involved in any choice you are making at this time. You will be better prepared when difficulty or danger strikes. Being prepared allows you to avoid the worst of it.

Third Line ━━━

Take some time before you act on what you have learned through this breakthrough. With the breakthrough comes an awareness, and with this awareness you will know what it is you need to do.

Fourth Line ━━━

This is a restless time for you. Be careful how you deal with this restlessness. Try to understand the cause of your restlessness. Is it simply time to move on? Are you bored and need something new to stimulate you? Are you actually upset about something and unsure as to what you can do about it? Is this the restlessness that comes with the teen years? You must name your restlessness correctly before you can do anything to remedy it.

Fifth Line ━━━━

You have some bad habits that need breaking or they will become who you are. In your teen years you are in the process of creating an adult from a child. What habits do you want to break before you enter your adult years? Some negative habits include putting people, including yourself, down; smoking cigarettes; and watching too much television. Learn to accept and befriend yourself and others, and these behaviors will transform into a lifetime of love and companionship.

Sixth Line ━━ ━━

Throughout the I Ching we are strongly counseled to be aware of this law: We reap what we sow. This is the natural and spiritual law of karma. If you plant a corn seed, corn will grow. If you plant an acorn, an oak tree will grow. If you plant love, love will grow. If you plant hate, . . .

Consider

Breakthroughs in thought are how many inventions and creations originate. Everything is a result of a breakthrough of some kind. When we become too inflexible in our ideas, or stuck in our assumptions, we lose the ability to be creative. Being flexible and open-minded lead to breakthroughs and opportunities. Sometimes it can help to read or listen to different points of view to stretch the mind. Public radio can be a great source of mind stretching. Search your radio for the local station and dare to listen to diverse points of view. While you listen, can you gain some understanding of a different point of view?

Life is a series of surprises.

—Ralph Waldo Emerson,
American essayist, poet, and spiritual philosopher

≡≡≡≡≡
≡≡≡≡≡
≡≡≡≡≡
≡≡≡≡≡
≡≡≡≡≡
≡≡ ≡≡

Heaven above

Wind below

44

Encounters

*I went so far past halfway I met myself
coming back.*
—Claudia Schmidt, folksinger and songwriter

Life is a series of encounters. What then makes up a healthy encounter? How can
we distinguish genuine interest from false interest? How might we know when someone is planning on taking advantage of us or has our best interest in mind? This
hexagram is about the importance of discerning our encounters and preventing a
harmful liaison. It is asking you, "*Who* are you encountering these days?"

This is the time to be particularly discriminating in all your encounters. Be ob-
servant of those who approach you, and ask yourself what their intents and motives
are. This does not mean that you need to be suspicious, only alert. Be flexible,
patient, and tolerant to all whom you encounter, while taking the time to discern
those you want to be with and those you do not. Make sure no one is trying to coax

you into something dangerous or harmful. The I Ching teaches us to meet others only *halfway*. This means that we shouldn't give up our principles or ideals to please someone else or to be accepted by someone. We are not meant to go beyond our own boundaries of what we know is right. We go past halfway when we put all the effort into making the relationship work, or when we give up parts of ourselves to be in a relationship.

Be particularly careful around those who make promises too easily to you or flatter you. What is it that they want and expect in return for these promises? This is also a time to be careful not to let others seduce you into a bad situation. In all your encounters now, don't rush anything. Tell others, "I will get back to you on that," when they try to force a commitment from you. Take your time, and give them an answer after you know what it is they expect from you and what you want from them.

First Line ▬ ▬

Negative emotions usually begin with a subtle mood. Do not build on these negative emotions by brooding over things. Use your inner strength to overcome them now, before they grow.

Second Line ▬▬▬

A dark mood is lingering. This is a good time to be kind to yourself. Give yourself the space to have these feelings without acting on them. Notice how these feelings are pushing you to act negatively. Simply observe these feelings, and the dark mood will pass.

Third Line ▬▬▬

Someone or something is causing you to want to argue or impress others. Wait until the need to argue passes and then, when calm, speak up.

Fourth Line ▬▬▬

You are working hard at being a better person, yet you witness others getting away with negative behaviors. This is a very good time to practice being nonjudgmental and tolerant. Tolerance of others brings you further peace. Remember: what they sow they will also reap.

Fifth Line ━━━━

You cannot prove yourself by putting others down. There is no gain in this, regardless of the situation. Kindness and tolerance bring the best results.

Sixth Line ━━━━

Either you are losing confidence in yourself or others are belittling you somehow. The best response is to withdraw and focus on the principles you know to be true. This situation will pass soon without your intervention.

Consider

The element of seduction in any kind of relationship is harmful. Seduction is an attempt to convince you of something that is not in your best interest. The statements used to convince you may be true—"You're beautiful," or "I can really appreciate how intelligent and creative you are"—but the speaker is not being honest about his or her *intent* with you. Seduction is always used when someone is trying to get something from you without being honest and clear about what it is they really want. For example, someone may say that you are beautiful or talented (and you are), but they really want to get some money from you or get you to have sex with them.

A good question to ask yourself in all encounters is: "Does this person care about me?" Practice asking that question from your heart rather than your head. Notice what you feel in your body when you're with this particular person and when you ask, "Is this person caring?" We often feel numb when we are being seduced, but other feelings may arise in the body as well, warning you that something isn't right.

If you are agreeing to being seduced, you are agreeing to give up something precious. What is it you are surrendering to this person?

Lake above

Earth below

45

Gathering Together

Everybody today seems to be in such a terrible rush, anxious for greater developments and greater riches and so on, so that children have very little time for their parents. Parents have very little time for each other, and in the home begins the disruption of the peace of the world.
—Mother Teresa, Catholic nun, winner of the Nobel Peace Prize

This hexagram is about how and why people gather in groups and the role you have in a group. Every group has a leader. Receiving this hexagram encourages you to develop your leadership skills. You must "gather together" the qualities of a skillful leader, so you may call others to do admirable things. Chances are people already look to you for ideas and guidance. The most powerful way to influence and lead others is to exhibit strong qualities oneself.

The more you develop a strong, honest, and good character, the more others will follow your example willingly. They will also listen to what you have to say and follow your advice, because they witness you living by what you say.

Being a leader means taking the time to be present in all your relationships. When you are too busy, have overcommitted, and can't get control of your time, all your relationships are diminished. In this case you need to "gather together" *yourself* in order to be present in your relationships and commitments.

It takes only one person to make great changes. It takes only one great leader to help gather people together. This time in your life is an ideal time to develop a healthy and strong attitude, to consider your choices, and to take risks that give you diverse experiences. This is a time in your life to develop your leadership skills. Your future depends upon the choices you make now.

First Line ▬▬ ▬▬

This is not the time to hesitate when you know what it is you need to do or say. Don't back off from your Inner Truth and principles. Be strong and sincere, and others will gather to you.

Second Line ▬▬ ▬▬

Remain open and gentle with yourself and others. Any kind of force will only increase the problem. Those who are intended to be together will be together without great effort on your part.

Third Line ▬▬ ▬▬

You can gather those you want around you at this time. Do this through patience, tolerance, and dependence on the wisdom of your Higher Power.

Fourth Line ▬▬▬▬

Do what's needed to benefit others and let go of wanting something in return. Great leaders sacrifice their own wants for the needs of others.

Fifth Line ▬▬▬▬

When gathering people together pay attention to their reasons for joining you. Are their reasons sincere? If not, the best way to deal with it is to further develop your own strengths and sincerity. As a result the negative effect will be small.

Sixth Line — — — —

Bringing people together is difficult, and you want to blame outside circumstances. Gather *yourself* together and reevaluate what needs to be done. Then some progress can be made.

Consider

What leaders inspire you? One reason they inspire you is that they reflect the traits that you are developing in yourself. Do these people quietly lead, or are they more outspoken? Read up on these people to learn more about the traits that you appreciate and are developing. If any of the leaders are deceased, such as Gandhi, watch a movie or documentary about this person; if alive, read up on this person's recent works in the papers. Let the developing leader in you resonate with the leaders you admire. This leader you admire could be local and someone you could interview.

You must be the change you wish to see in the world.
**—Mahatma Gandhi,
Indian nationalist and spiritual leader**

Earth above

Wind below

46

Becoming

Our deepest desire is to share our riches, and this desire is rooted in the dynamics of the cosmos. What began as an outward expansion of the universe in the fireball, ripens into your desire to flood all things with goodness. Whenever you are filled with a desire to fling your gifts into the world, you have become the cosmic dynamic of celebration, feeling its urgency to pour forth just as the stars felt the same urgency to pour themselves out.
—Thomas Berry, American poet, author of *The Dream of the Earth*

This hexagram is about that which is ascending, moving upward. For you it holds the message of Becoming. You are becoming the person you were intended to become the moment you were born. You are becoming an independent adult through

these intense teen years. These years hold within them the energy of becoming unlike any you will ever have again in your life.

The image associated with this hexagram is that of a tree pushing upward through the earth. (The lower trigram, wind, is also identified as wood in many translations.) When a tree is pushing itself through the earth, most of its energy needs to be used for this purpose. It would not make it if it were to get distracted from its purpose of Becoming. Similarly, a great deal of your energy needs to be involved in your Becoming process. Be careful not get too distracted from this objective. It takes a balanced attitude to remain focused on Becoming. Too much shopping, eating, getting high, surfing the Internet, competitive sports, and obsessing about romantic relationships distract us from our Becoming.

Are you putting enough time into your Becoming? Are you finding that you are putting too much time into something that is taking away from your growth? Sometimes we are too distracted with how we look or appear and lose sight of what brings lasting happiness. Eating disorders are an example of how we get misdirected from the true process of Becoming and too involved in appearing a certain way.

This is a sacred and special time of your life.

First Line ━━ ━━

Be confident and strong in your natural abilities. There are those who want to help you bring forth these gifts of yours. You are meant to bring your gifts into the world, and become who you are.

Second Line ━━━━

Develop the qualities of sincerity and truthfulness, for these will result in a life of joy. You may be called upon to be sincere and truthful with someone now; this will further your Becoming and increase your happiness.

Third Line ━━━━

During this time in your life, a great vast unknown spreads before you. You are Becoming, but what are you becoming, and what lies ahead for you really? Trust in the journey and the help of your Higher Power.

Fourth Line ━━ ━━

Your sincerity and trust in a Higher Power have brought you much happiness.

Fifth Line ━━ ━━

Most changes and growth are made in gradual steps and not rushed. The way to Become is to proceed step-by-step, not trying to rush through your teen years. Disaster results when we try to rush things in nature. Honor the time and effort it takes to become the adult you are growing into. And take time to just hang out and play.

Sixth Line ━━ ━━

Throughout the process of Becoming, you need to pay attention to when there are opportunities and when there are not. When the door is closed, accept this and move on. Opportunity will come again.

Consider

Make a collage of your Becoming. Gather pictures, words, photos, poetry, and cards that represent who you are becoming. Find a bulletin board to display the collage. Hang it in a place where you can add to it as you continue to find things. Some teens use an entire wall in their room as a background for their collages.

Who will make us laugh and love?
Maybe mothers loving babies
Maybe gentle eyes that see.
Or beyond the other maybes
Maybe you and maybe me.
**—James Kavanaugh, poet,
from *Who Will Make the City Joyful?***

Lake above

Water below

47

Exhaustion

*. . . my
jaws ache for release, for
words that will say*

*anything. I force myself
to remember
who I am, what I am, and
      why I am here . . .*
—Philip Levine, author, from *Finding What You Didn't Lose*

You're exhausted. It's time to give in to your fatigue and rest. Rest is a necessary part of creativity and life. The image is of an empty or dried-up lake. The water has been completely used up. If you resist or deny yourself this rest, you will only become more exhausted and likely become sick. Accomplishing much simply isn't

possible right now. Can you let go of needing to push yourself? This may mean letting go of the fear that you are going to miss something. You need to take care of yourself now, so future opportunities aren't missed.

Receiving this hexagram could also be a warning that you've gone too far with something and need to take a break from it. Continuing to push yourself would only further exhaust you and could result in a depression. When exhausted, you need to be careful not to let negative emotions and attitudes take over. People are more vulnerable to negative feelings when tired. It is time to rest and regain some physical and spiritual strength.

First Line ━━ ━━

The situation on the outside will improve when you improve your internal environment: your attitude, feelings, and beliefs. Practice having a more positive attitude while at the same time accepting the situation as it is.

Second Line ━━━━

The world has weighed heavy on your heart and you're feeling tired. Be careful not to become too impatient with yourself or others. When your heart is heavy, it's a good time to be kind to yourself and take a break from things.

Third Line ━━ ━━

Stop trying to force things to be better. Focus instead on the blessings you do have. You are too fatigued to handle difficulties well.

Fourth Line ━━━━

Turn to your Higher Power for help. You are starting to be hard on yourself, and this only hinders your progress. Being too tired to do certain things is simply the body's way of telling you to slow down. Accept this time with grace.

Fifth Line ━━━━

No matter how much effort you put into being a good person, life at times becomes burdensome. Life is formidable right now. Don't make it all about yourself.

Sixth Line ━━ ━━

Having thoughts that you will never succeed only feeds the exhaustion. Such negative thoughts are like creeping vines that slowly cover a window and block out the sunlight. Don't let them take over; things can and will work out. Get some rest.

Consider

Focusing on your blessings is a good way to rest. Before you go to bed each night review your blessings. Rest in the gratitude and awareness of your many blessings, whatever they may be.

There are different ways to understand exhausting. One can become exhausted by not having enough, or by having too much. When one is stuck in an exhausting situation, it is wise to discover the cause and seek the solution. That is what the wise do. Merely complaining and being resentful will only make the situation worse.

—Taoist Master Alfred Huang,
from *The Complete I Ching*, hexagram 47

Water above

Wind below

48

Well-being

Everything in nature invites us constantly to be what we are. We are often like rivers: careless and forceful, timid and dangerous, lucid and muddied, eddying, gleaming, still.
—Gretel Ehrlich, author of *The Solace of Open Spaces*

The image of this hexagram is of a well. A well, particularly in small villages, is a place of refreshment and water. In such villages the people have their marketplace around the well. Maintaining the village well, their only supply of water, was of the greatest importance. The water in a well, like the wisdom of the I Ching, is an inexhaustible resource.

There is something in each of us that always acts as a source of strength. Some people refer to this part as our "soul," "inner self," "psyche," "authentic self," or

Well-being

"True Nature." Whatever we call it, it is a place we can go to get replenished; it is a source of well-being. It is our internal well, and this source is inexhaustible.

There is an abundance of underground streams that we tap in to by digging wells. To reach the source of strength and nourishment inside ourselves, we also have to dig. Receiving this hexagram should encourage you to take the time to check in with the state of your inner being. What is the state of your well, your soul? Are you doing things that help you come in contact with this source of wisdom and strength, such as meditating and living creatively and harmlessly? Or are you engaging in activities and thoughts that are damaging the well? This is the time to review how you are treating yourself—whether or not you are contributing to your well-being.

First Line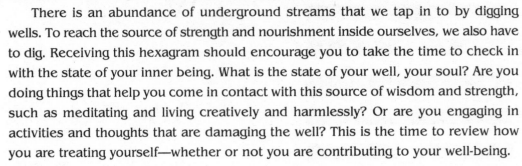

When you don't respect and care for yourself, others will not respect you either. It is time for you to take a serious look at how your life is developing. Are you neglecting yourself and damaging your well-being?

Second Line

You are being too careless with your life. Can you feel the effects of this on your body, mind, and spirit? These are the years that you are digging your well and reaching to that place of self-nourishment. Use these years wisely by taking care of yourself, and you will benefit your entire life.

Third Line

You have many gifts to offer but are not putting them to use. Everyone loses when you disregard your gifts. This neglect diminishes your sense of well-being. Bring forth your gifts, and everyone will benefit.

Fourth Line

Attend to your well-being. You have not yet learned to draw enough "water from the well" (wisdom and strength from your own inner source). The teen years are the time to prepare for your future by building up your inner resources.

Fifth Line ━━━

You hold great potential for yourself and your community. You have the strength and knowledge of a good person. Draw from this strength and knowledge now to help you through this situation. All will work out.

Sixth Line ━━ ━━

Because you are a compassionate and open-minded person, you are learning to become a source of well-being for your family and community. This compassionate heart of yours will bring you great love and happiness.

Consider

Join up with someone who will help you to strengthen and build upon your well-being. A therapist can help you dig to the source within yourself, as can a good mentor, spiritual advisor, or meditation teacher. If you received changing lines 1 through 4, seek the help of a good therapist. What makes a good therapist? Consider these questions in your first session with a therapist. Remember: you get to choose who you want to work with.

• Will she answer your questions about therapy; about herself? If she is not open to you asking questions, consider finding someone else.

• Is he respectful? Does he focus his attention on you? Or is he too involved in writing notes? Therapists don't need to write notes during sessions—they can do this afterward.

• Is she flexible and open to new ideas? Does she have some knowledge about the things you are interested in?

• Does he enjoy being a therapist? You can ask this, or observe this in how he behaves. An unhappy therapist

 1   is not responsive or interested in you or your requests (you feel put off);

 2. appears tired, disinterested, and bored;

 3. lacks a sense of humor

4.   lacks a true sense of curiosity about you and what you are saying;

5.   speaks judgmentally about you or others;

6.   appears distracted;

7.   doesn't express happiness in what she or he is doing; and

8.   complains about things to you.

- How do you feel in her office? Check in with your body and emotions. Does the office environment feel good, safe, open?

Water in a stream is a gift of nature. Water in a well results from the accomplishment of human beings. All the underground streams are there, but without digging the water is wasted.

—Taoist Master Alfred Huang,
from *The Complete I Ching*, hexagram 48

```
▬▬▬▬    ▬▬▬▬
▬▬▬▬▬▬▬▬▬▬▬▬
▬▬▬▬▬▬▬▬▬▬▬▬
▬▬▬▬▬▬▬▬▬▬▬▬
▬▬▬▬    ▬▬▬▬
▬▬▬▬▬▬▬▬▬▬▬▬
```

Lake above

Fire below

49

Coming-of-Age

Toto, I've a feeling we're not in Kansas anymore.
—Dorothy, from *The Wizard of Oz*

*Through metaphor we pass from one state of
knowing into the next, ever experimenting, ever
creating, ever flowing, as the universe does. It is
our state of seeing that makes roses bloom—in
aprons, on paper, on frozen life paths. Sometimes
this state comes about through a willful creative
leap, sometimes it arrives as a gift of grace.*
**—Burghild Nina Holzer, author of *A Walk Between Heaven and Earth:
A Personal Journal on Writing and the Creative Process***

Big changes are on the horizon. Your ideas, relationships, and body all are meta-
morphosing into a young adult—you are coming of age. Something at this time is

bringing this change to the forefront of your life. As the old breaks away, room is made for the new that's coming into your life. This passage from childhood to adulthood, the teen years, is known as the coming-of-age years. Change occurs at a rapid rate, pulling us away from the old and making room for all that's developing in you. You receive this hexagram because you are making improvements that are helping you with this passage. You are in touch with the importance of this time of life and are using it to its fullest. You have opened yourself to transformative changes, and these changes are taking place now.

Such life changes can be so intense that they begin to throw you off balance. Try to stay balanced by noticing how your choices affect you and others. Enjoy and use this transformative time to evolve into the kind of adult you want to be. Those around you are feeling the positive effects of this change; they see the adult emerging. Keep yourself balanced and maintain your integrity, and the coming-of-age will be filled with blessings.

First Line ━━━

You have begun to come of age. This is the process of your Becoming (hexagram 46) and is not dependent on your chronological age. Many people who are late in life have never really come of age! Act wisely, and wait until the most favorable time to move forward. Some patience is needed.

Second Line ━━ ━━

If you first prepare yourself with a ritual (see the following box), you will be ready to take the necessary steps. Once you have made your decision to move forward, do not second guess yourself or become arrogant. Be humble about this progress.

Third Line ━━━

This is the time to act, but act only after great consideration. Ask yourself what childhood characteristics or choices need to be let go of now.

Fourth Line ━━━

Great and enduring changes are dependent on your inner attitude and how you treat others. If you hold on to a negative attitude and mistreat others, the positive change that is present now will not last.

Fifth Line ━━━━━

Due to the fact that you live by the higher principles of truthfulness, compassion, and kindness, the positive change continues and others come to respect you.

Sixth Line ━━ ━━

The present change is coming to an end (you will experience many coming-of-age experiences throughout this passage into your adult years), and success is assured as long as you maintain your high principles.

Consider

Read about or get help planning a coming-of-age ritual for yourself and some of your peers. An initiation ceremony (hexagram 1) can be part of your coming-of-age ceremony, or it can be a separate ceremony. If you haven't had any kind of coming-of-age ritual or acknowledgment, consider having one now. Western cultures lost this valuable rite of passage and are only recently bringing it back. Refer to thunderingyears.com Web site for additional resources.

Jacob's Coming-of-Age Ritual

Jacob planned his coming-of-age ceremony with his mentor, stepfather, and mother. He wanted it to represent his Native American roots, yet not be too complicated. He also wanted to receive a spiritual (Native American) name. So his mentor helped set up a sweat lodge with Jacob and six of his male friends. They invited a local Native American elder who facilitated the sweat with the boys and Jacob's mentor.

After the sweat they slept under the stars for a vision for Jacob. They gathered the next morning around a fire built by the elder and the mentor. Jacob was given his spiritual name by the elder and gifts from his friends. They all shared the experiences they had under the stars, along with their visions for Jacob. All of them expressed an interest in having their own coming-of-age rituals. Afterward, all the mothers and others from the community prepared a big meal, during which Jacob was welcomed back into the community as a man.

Fire above

Wind below

50
The Cauldron

The Celtic afterworld is called the Land of Youth, and the secret that opens its door is found in the cauldron: The secret of immortality lies in seeing death as an integral part of the cycle of life. Nothing is ever lost from the universe: Rebirth can be seen in life itself, where every ending brings a new beginning.
—Starhawk, ritualist, peace activist, and author of *The Spiral Dance*

The symbol for this hexagram is one of a sacred vessel, a cauldron, which holds a long history of holy significance to cultures around the world. In Chinese tradition the cauldron symbolizes the importance of nourishing the ancestors (the spiritual source) so the entire community will be blessed. It speaks to the importance of showing our spiritual source appreciation for its help in our lives. The ultimate show of appreciation is how we live our own lives.

At this time you need to prepare your sacred vessel—your life—for all that wants to enter into it. Preparing for your life is like sending a request for what you would like your future to hold out to the world (universe). You will get back what you prepare for. As a teenager, whatever you do now is basically preparation for your entire adult life, one reason that this time is so valuable. What do you want to invite into your vessel? What are you "cooking" in your cauldron? The thoughts you hold on to, the ideas you create, the dreams you dream, the plans you make, the relationships you foster are all cooked in your cauldron. So ask yourself what it is that you are bringing into your life as you open more and more to the adult that is emerging.

First Line ▬ ▬

Now is the time to clean up your act, or in this case your "cauldron." You don't want to cook sacred food in a polluted vessel. End any harmful relationships and stop abusing drugs or engaging in any destructive behaviors. Stop focusing on negative thoughts. Prepare yourself for the good that is coming into your life by making room for it.

Second Line ▬▬

Choose your friends carefully and wisely. You are establishing the qualities of a mature and spiritually based person. Others may try to distract you from this path (we all encounter those who do). They may be jealous of your success. Choose to associate only with those who support and encourage your efforts and successes.

Third Line ▬▬

You are temporarily blocked by something. If you can be patient during this time of obstruction it will quickly pass. If the block is internal you will need to identify it and be willing to make the necessary attitude adjustment. You will find happiness.

Fourth Line ▬▬

Don't take your spiritual responsibilities too lightly. Be respectful of how you use the guidance you receive from the I Ching. If you get righteous you will bring trouble on yourself. You get righteous by trying to convert others to your way of life.

Fifth Line — —

Make the most of the situation. Can you find a balanced way of taking advantage of this opportunity? If you are balanced in your approach, everything will naturally, and in time, fall into place.

Sixth Line ———

"Do unto others as you would have others do unto you": a golden rule that comes up in all the world's spiritual traditions. Live by this golden rule, and everything will turn out beneficially.

Consider

Find a vessel or a cauldron. You could use a cauldron found in nature, such as an opening in the ground or a tree, or an iron cauldron of any size. Once you find a cauldron, do the following cauldron meditation,

Place your face about six inches away from the cauldron's opening. If it is a very large cauldron, sit beside it. Ground yourself (see hexagram 15), and look into the opening of the cauldron. Imagine the power of this space. Think of yourself as such a sacred cauldron. Acknowledge your life and all you bring into it as a sacred journey. The journey is still new. What do you want to cook in this sacred cauldron? Imagine filling this cauldron with all that you want to offer the ancestors and all that you want to invite into your life, and offer it to your spiritual source. Imagine the power and potential you are calling into the cauldron. Fill yourself with this power and potential. When you are finished, sit quietly for a few moments. Offer some gratitude for all that was available to you to place in your cauldron.

Thunder above

Thunder below

51

The Thunderers

Once the spring thunder bursts, myriad beings on earth are awakened.
—Chinese proverb

In many Native American traditions the thunderbird symbolizes the energy of thunder (as does this hexagram). You are meant to thunder at this time in your life. You are meant to make adults and the community uncomfortable with your sounds. You are meant to make us all take notice. You then bring to your life and your community the rains of change. From thunder comes life-giving rains. You are meant to bring life-giving rains to the community. You can, and should, do this without causing any harm. This hexagram encourages you to act out, speak up, and disrupt the status quo.

In many I Ching translations this hexagram is called "shock." Your teenage energy is a necessary shock to the community. Let yourself thunder and shock with your creative and assertive energy. Don't go along with the crowd or a gang for comfort's sake. You may receive this hexagram when others are having trouble with your intense energy, or when you need to harness it more creatively. Act out with compassion. Cause no one harm. Disrupt the status quo with an open and kind heart.

First Line ━━━━

Acting out, shocking others, and making people uncomfortable with your beliefs is not wrong or bad. Don't let anyone tell you that speaking out is wrong. Others are meant to learn from you and will come to understand this in time.

Second Line ━━ ━━

The shocking event is already having its effect on you and others. If you have caused harm in any way, admit it and repair the damage. Learn from this experience so you won't repeat it. This is an opportunity to learn from your mistake.

Third Line ━━ ━━

When you act outrageously without causing any harm, you startle and shock others, but they also learn from you. People take notice and listen.

Fourth Line ━━━━

You or someone else in your life is "stuck in the mud." This is not the time to continue acting out. Be still, and wait for events to change of their own accord. If you fight further, you will only become more mired in the mud.

Fifth Line ━━ ━━

This is not a productive time. The shock has been turned on you, and presently you are thrown off balance. The best thing to do is remain strong and centered. Rethink how you might approach the same situation more effectively. You will be okay.

Sixth Line ━━ ━━

You have really upset the apple cart this time! That's okay, but recognize that it's time to back off and let everyone handle the shock in their own way. Others may be fearful of you, or you may be the object of gossip. Don't interfere. You have plenty of other things to focus on.

Consider

How can you act out and speak up without causing harm? Is there someone you want to speak up to but hesitate because they have authority over you? There is no law that says you can't be honest with someone who sits in a seat of authority. Just proceed in a respectful and cautious manner.

Also Consider

In Native American mythology thunderbirds are the personification of thunder. They create thunder by moving their wings. They make lightning by opening and shutting their eyes. In the Lakota tradition, those who become *heyoka* (dream interpreters) do so because they have dreamed of the thunderbirds.

Are your dreams in any way stirring you up? Do you believe you receive any insights or messages within your dreams? Sometimes when we are not speaking up about something in our waking lives, the issue becomes bigger in our dreams. Are the thunderbirds talking to you? Start paying more attention to your dreams.

Mountain above

Mountain below

52

Being Still

*All human evil comes from a single cause: man's
inability to sit still in a room.*
—Blaise Pascal, seventeenth-century French scientist and philosopher

Be still, and know that I am God.
—Psalms 46:10

Receiving this hexagram indicates that you need to make meditation a regular part
of your life. Since ancient times, meditation (becoming still) has been understood
as necessary for a healthy and happy life. To be still means to quiet the body, mind,
and spirit. All Wisdomkeepers are great meditators, for they know that the quiet but
strong voice of wisdom comes to a still mind. Meditation nourishes the mind, body,
and spirit. No matter what your spiritual beliefs and practices, meditation will enrich

it. To meditate means to become still and alert like a mountain. The image is of a mountain on mountain. Like a mountain, you sit and watch the "stream" (breath). Meditation prepares your mind and spirit for upcoming events.

As we still our minds and take the time to meditate, we become more in tune with times of opportunity and times of adversity. When we are caught up in our own thoughts, we often lose sight of what is really going on around us. Sometimes the door is open and a person is receptive to us; other times the door is closed. In Master Huang's commentary on this hexagram he states: "The key to success is to advance when it is time to advance and to stop when it is time to stop."

Receiving this hexagram also suggests that you need to rest your mind, still your mind, because you are becoming overwhelmed with thoughts. Stephen Levine, a great meditation teacher, believes that thoughts are our greatest addictions! We are so attached to what we think that we have a very difficult time not thinking. And too often this thinking consists of worrying or ruminating. Can you "flow like the stream"? Can you relax your thoughts and take the time to meditate?

First Line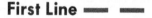

Rest and be still. Receiving this line means that you need to stop and look before you jump into something. Things will work out if you take this precaution.

Second Line ━━ ━━

Be careful whose advice you follow. Always be true to yourself, and wait for a better time to take action. It is best to remain still even though others are taking action.

Third Line ━━━━

Practicing meditation helps you handle your intense feelings without having to react to them. Through the practice of meditation, learn to experience your feelings without allowing them to control you. Restless feelings are on the rise; be still and strong, and don't react. After you've obtained peace of mind, you will know what the best action is.

Fourth Line —— ——

When you are full of fear and doubt, it is not the time to take action. Meditation can help you reach a place of peace and clarity. Then it will be time to act.

Fifth Line —— ——

Wait before you speak up. Once something is said it can't be taken back. Remember that words have impact. Be still, gain some clarity, and then speak your mind.

Sixth Line ————

Developing a meditation practice and a compassionate heart will bring a lifetime of happiness. Remain true to such a path and nothing will disrupt your peace of mind.

Basic Mindfulness Meditation

This may be read aloud slowly or taped and listened to.

Continue to sit comfortably, yet alert . . . holding your body in the meditative posture, like a mountain . . . alert and tall. Slowly close your eyes and begin to let go of the experiences, thoughts, and expectations you brought with you. . . . Let go . . . softening around the moods, experiences, and thoughts. Let them come . . . and let them go . . . like waves of an ocean. Allow yourself to be fully present for this practice of meditation, letting go of worries you may have been carrying with you. As you notice what's present—the thoughts that are on your mind, or the physical sensations that are rising and falling in your body—let them come and go as they will. Get a sense of the container called "the body." Notice the physical sensations of this meditating body. Get an overall sense of this body sitting. Try to not hold on to any thoughts, but let them go. As you do this, become aware of your breathing.

Notice that in the middle of all these thoughts and feelings there is a soft sensation of breathing. Now bring your attention to this breathing. . . . Letting the breath flow by itself, notice the physical sensations of breath, the coolness of the in-breath and warmth of the out-breath brushing against the top of your nostrils, or the rise and fall of your belly as you breathe. Notice the physical sensation of breath as it moves in your body. Let yourself

feel your life-giving breath. Rest in the breathing. Rest in the meditating body. . . . Bring your awareness gently to it. . . .

Keep some of your awareness on the body as it continues to sit alert and tall. Be aware of this body meditating. Maintain some of your awareness on the body as you bring most of your attention to your breath. . . .

After just a few breaths you will notice that a thought carries you off on its own wave of experience and feeling. Notice where this wave of thought has taken you; let your awareness go there, then gently return your awareness back to the breath and to this meditating body. Rest again and again in the breath by gently focusing your attention on the physical sensations of your breath . . . letting the breath flow through you, naturally. Hold a mindful attention on your breath, noticing when your attention moves away on another wave of thought or physical sensation, returning your awareness to the sensations of your breathing and the body meditating.

Now, when you are ready to stop meditating, gently bring your awareness to your entire body. Feel the body sitting in its upright, meditative mountain posture. . . . as you gently open your eyes and refocus your attention on your environment.

The seed of mystery lies in muddy water.
How can I perceive this mystery?
Water becomes clear through stillness.
How can I become still?
By flowing with the stream.
— Lao-tzu, ancient Taoist sage
and author of *Tao-te Ching*

Wind* above

Mountain below

53

What's the Rush?

If you want to be happy, be.
—Ralph Waldo Emerson, American essayist, poet, and spiritual philosopher

*There is no royal road to anything. One thing at a
time, and all things in succession. That which grows
slowly endures.*
—Josiah Holland, author of *Lessons in Life*

The image that accompanies this hexagram is that of a tree growing high on a
mountain. As the tree on the mountaintop grows, it also sends its roots deep into
the mountain. It's a process that cannot be rushed. This reflects the wisdom found
in nature: that which is strong and stable became that way *gradually*, and it takes

---

*This trigram or gua is both wind or wood element. In this hexagram it is best understood as
wood.

balanced growth inward and outward to create a tall, strong tree (life). When we rush things we tend to skip important steps and miss valuable opportunities. What you need to do now is persevere and take the necessary steps. For example, when we rush into a relationship, especially a marriage, it often results in disappointment. When we rush things it is usually due to hidden fears about what we think might or might not happen.

With regard to your inquiry, it is important to take the step-by-step approach. Copy nature, and persevere to the end. Even though you want to rush the process, slow down and appreciate each step that needs to be taken. There is a succession to all things, and when we are moving too fast we lose touch with this natural sequence. Try to tap in to the natural order and timing of what you're inquiring about, and in so doing you will experience a natural and beautiful outcome.

First Line ▬ ▬

The initial stages of growth are often the most vulnerable. The roots are not yet deep. Likewise, a new relationship needs to develop slowly. Progress naturally without trying to rush things and happiness will come to you.

Second Line ▬ ▬

When good comes to you, share the success and happiness with others. A tree does not hoard the sun. Share your prosperity and happiness and it will increase.

Third Line ▬▬▬

You are considering or have begun to go against your intuition. Your intuition knows not to rush things or to assume too much. Receiving this line indicates that you may be pushing a relationship that is not in your best interest. Once you become aware of this, change your course of action with this person. A lasting friendship later on is possible.

Fourth Line ▬ ▬

You have encountered some difficulty. Do not fight against it. Let things evolve naturally, and the situation will unfold in a good way.

Fifth Line ━━━━

You are making progress in your personal and spiritual development. This may bring on the envy of others who compare themselves to you. Be tolerant of them while not letting their attitudes jar you off your course. By remaining true to yourself and your path you will have success.

Sixth Line ━━━━

漸

As a result of your own gradual progress, you obtain the help of your Higher Power. Others are inspired by your example.

Consider

Slow progress can be frustrating. You want success, love, happiness, recognition, and money *now*. You want the relationship to move to the next step. You want to be finished with something *today*.

There is nothing wrong with wanting all these things. The challenge is, can you hold on to all these desires, keep them as something you are moving *toward*, but return your attention to what is needed at the moment? Can you turn your focus to the next step instead of the desired outcome? Treat the outcome as something you are moving toward, such as a beautiful distant horizon, while keeping most of your attention on the next step. The desired outcome becomes something that motivates you instead of distracting you from the necessary step-by-step process.

Thunder above

Lake below

54

Being Undermined

Something we were withholding made us weak,
Until we found it was ourselves.
—Robert Frost, American poet

You are in a position in which you cannot influence others, and you are likely being undermined. You don't feel heard or noticed, because you are not valued in this particular relationship. Even though you are contributing to the situation, your talents are not being recognized. You may have agreed to something that turns out not to be such a good idea. If you are inquiring about a relationship, be careful about what you are agreeing to (or what you have agreed to already). Are you agreeing because of flattery and confusing this with real love? Is this person expecting things of you too soon, or requesting you to give up everything for him or her? Just because you are attracted to someone doesn't mean that he or she is the right person for you. Receiving this hexagram is a warning that you may be in danger of giving up your principles to be in a relationship.

You need to decide how you want to be treated by others, and allow relationships to develop *before* committing to them. It is okay to require that others prove themselves worthy of your commitment and love.

This hexagram is also about knowing how to handle yourself once you find yourself in a compromising position. Although you have no power to change others, you can influence them (although this influence may take time). Through the power of Inner Truth, independence, and compassion for yourself, you have a positive influence on the situation.

First Line ━━━━

You have little influence at this time. Take a position in the background, and things will work out.

Second Line ━━━━

Do not lose your self-confidence because of the limiting circumstances. Focus on the good in yourself, others, and the situation. Even though the situation appears to be hopeless, a happy ending is possible.

Third Line ━━ ━━

There's nothing to do now but wait. You will discover the success in this tactic at a later time. Persevere.

Fourth Line ━━━━

It is worth waiting for the right person before making a long-term commitment. Also, it is better to decide about your sexual boundaries before entering a relationship. Do you have to be sexually intimate with someone to have a serious commitment?

Fifth Line ━━ ━━

Put spiritual principles first; all else will then follow in a good way.

Sixth Line ━━ ━ ━

Receiving this line is a reminder that honesty and respect need to be the foundation for all your relationships. Is there someone you need to be truthful with? Or, is there someone deceiving you?

Consider

"The Wolf and the Heron," *Aesop's Fables*

A wolf, eating too quickly, swallowed a large bone that then got stuck in his throat. He wandered around in search of someone to help him get it out. Finally, he met up with a heron, who had a long beak for catching fish, and asked her to pull the bone out of his throat. The wolf promised her a great reward in exchange for her help.

She agreed and stuck her long beak and then her entire head into the throat of the wolf and pulled out the bone.

"I got it," said the heron. "Now give me my reward."

"My dear friend, after putting your head in the mouth of a wolf, you should be happy that I didn't bite it off. What more would you expect?"

55

Abundance

Everybody, sooner or later, sits down to a banquet of consequences.
—Robert Louis Stevenson, Scottish essayist, novelist, and poet

The image of this hexagram is that of thunder and lightning—intense energy. Having intense energy can yield abundance in many forms: ideas, friends, creativity, opportunities, influence, money, or experiences. Use this time well, and it will return again and again.

You are likely to experience many times of abundance—thunder and lightning—throughout your teen years. This is how it is meant to be. You should use this intense energy to propel you through your teen years and into your adult years. You are intended to influence the changes in your life, and those in your community, with this energy and abundance. The energy of the teen years is unique and power-

ful. It also holds lasting spiritual significance, because how you use this time in your life will have a great influence on the rest of your life.

Times of great abundance arrive when we cultivate skills such as compassion, inner independence, courage, and mindfulness. However, as with everything, this abundance is limited, and in this case short-lived. So, enjoy it while it lasts. Be careful not to exceed the limits of this abundance by overcommitting or overspending, for example. Also, be prepared for the "down time" when the abundance has come full circle and is ending. It is a natural cycle, but it may feel like a letdown. Things cannot always remain in great abundance.

First Line ━━━

Pay attention to the synchronicity (meaningful coincidences) in your life (see the following box).

Second Line ━━ ━

There are others who mistrust or envy your time of abundance. There is nothing you can do about them at this time. Hold on to your beliefs.

Third Line ━━━

Your abundance is making others' egos rise, and now they want to prove themselves. Trust in your Higher Power and the situation will improve. You are doing nothing wrong.

Fourth Line ━━━

Seek and nurture healthy relationships. Who you are in relationships with says a lot about who you are and what you will become. Connect with those who can help and support you.

Fifth Line ━━ ━

The spiritual path is continually filled with blessings. Follow the guidance of the I Ching, your Higher Power, and your Inner Truth and more abundance is assured.

Sixth Line — —

There is no more room for further abundance. Use your abundance lovingly and wisely and happiness will endure beyond this time of great abundance.

Consider

Notice synchronicity in your life. Synchronicity is a way Spirit speaks to us and helps us out. It is a way Spirit says to us, "Yes, you are on the correct path," or grabs your attention and says, "Consider this!" Synchronistic events include chance encounters with people you've been thinking about and waking events matching dreams. Most often it is an event that coincides with a thought or dream.

For example, once I had just gone into the admissions office to see if I could attend the university that fall. They told me I didn't have enough algebra credits. I had attended an alternative free school and my records there didn't show enough algebra credits. I couldn't get into the university without these math credits. I was very upset and disappointed. I felt that I was on the correct path—I wanted to go on to school and had real plans of what I was going to do with my degrees. I thought God was behind me on this one, but now I started to wonder. What was I going to do now?

Upset and discouraged, I went to the local coffeehouse, sat down, and began to drink a soda at the counter. My eyes were on my lap. Then, I happened to look up . . . and guess who was sitting next to me? My high school math teacher! (Good thing I looked up.) I told him what had just happened and how much I wanted to attend the university. He said that he would send a letter confirming that I did indeed take enough algebra credits. I was then accepted into the university, and now, thirty years later, I am able to write this book.

I've experienced simpler synchronicity, such as thinking of a friend and then she calls, or being told by three different people about a book I should read and then someone else gives me the book as a gift, or dreaming about someone and then running into him.

Where and how is synchronicity showing up in your life? Synchronicity is always happening, because Spirit always wants to help us. We just have to pay attention, look up from our laps, and see who is sitting next to us.

Fire above

Mountain below

56

The Traveler

We can never bathe twice in the same river.
—Heracleitus, ancient Greek philosopher

It is time to move forward. Perhaps something has come to an end, and you need to let it go and move on. Life is a series of changes, so it is important for each of us to know how to travel through all the changes that arise. Many good things happen, but we need to let these go and move on to the next experience. We often try to hold on to the good things longer than they are intended to last. Difficult times occur too, and we need to travel through these as well. "We can never bathe twice in the same river," because the river is *always moving!* Even when we return to the same place to swim, the water is new. Accept that your teen years are a fairly rapid succession of new things. Learning to be a good "traveler" will help you enjoy this time more.

You are, ultimately, *traveling* through your teen years. Perhaps you want to get these years over with and move on to your adult years, or maybe you don't want them ever to end! The reality is, they take as long as they take. Receiving this hexagram can mean that you need to enjoy the teen years and all they have to offer without trying to rush through them or hold on to them. Acknowledge yourself as a traveler traveling through these intense teen years and through life.

This hexagram is also about trusting the unknown. Accept that there is a lot we don't know (about our futures, our Higher Power, Spirit, ourselves). Ultimately every day holds immense possibility! When we get too set in our ways of thinking or behaving, we can miss many great opportunities. Knowing that we can't "bathe in the same river twice" means that each experience, each moment, holds something new within it. Trust in the mystery, that which is unknown, relying on your Higher Power as the perfect traveling companion. This time in your life is so full of changes! Open yourself to each experience and relationship and to the potential they hold for you.

First Line ▬ ▬

When you set your sights low and expect little of yourself, that is what you tend to get back. Don't limit yourself. Open up to all the myriad possibilities life is offering you now as a teenager.

Second Line ▬ ▬

Others want to help you when you are kind and thoughtful of them. Practice going into each new experience with an open heart.

Third Line ▬▬▬

You either have or are considering meddling into someone else's affairs, which are not your concern. This will result in a negative situation unless you change course quickly. Treat others with respect, and they will respect you.

Fourth Line ▬▬▬

You have already gotten caught up in fears and doubts. Work on settling your thoughts, and the situation will improve.

Fifth Line ▬ ▬

Your recent concern is coming to an end. Although there has been some difficulty, your efforts to do the right thing have brought you success. You are likely being recognized for your good efforts.

Sixth Line ▬▬▬

Be careful not to let your successes go to your head. Enjoy them fully, but be generous to others who are not experiencing such success. If you become too self-centered, you can lose what you've achieved.

Consider

Meditate on the law of change—of impermanence. This law shows that everything is always in a state of change. Even diamonds don't last forever. To meditate on this law, quietly consider how everything changes; nothing remains the same. To realize this creates more peace and happiness in our lives, because we stop trying to make the good times last or stop trying too hard to avoid the difficult times. We can't always feel good, but our sad feelings won't last forever either. When we are in the natural flow of this law, we are happier, because then we are in the natural flow of life. We let change happen. We let ourselves move through our teen years, enjoying all the wonderful times, and getting through the more difficult ones.

Everything is in flux.

—Heracleitus,
ancient Greek philosopher

Wind above

Wind below

57

Running a Marathon

*One of the simplest things about all the facts of life
is that to get where you want to go, you must keep
on going.*
—Norman Vincent Peale, American clergyman and author

*Energy follows intent, so be mindful of your
intentions.*
—Colleen Brenzy, healer and philosopher

You are in need of the energy and the focus it takes to run a marathon. This means that it is important for you to keep your attention on the goal, to steady your pace and keep moving. If you push too hard in the beginning you will not make it to the finish line. A marathon is something you also need to prepare for months in ad-

vance. An enduring, flexible, and strong mind and body will be what helps you in this situation.

No matter what this situation is about, you need to be prepared in order to hang in there for the long haul. Reserve your energy so you will have what it takes to persevere to the end. Remember that influencing others also requires a slow and steady approach.

Be conscious of your intent for this situation. What is it you hope to get out of it? What is your purpose? Do you intend to follow through to the end? If you have prepared for this situation (marathon) and your intent (to finish the race) is strong and clear, you will succeed.

First Line ▬▬ ▬▬

When you know that you are prepared and you have put aside your doubts and fears, move forward. Remain focused on your goal.

Second Line ▬▬▬▬

Look for hidden agendas. You would benefit from the help of a counselor or mentor to get beyond what threatens you now. In this case it is helpful to understand the intent of everyone involved in the situation.

Third Line ▬▬▬▬

Focus on the goal, but don't worry about the outcome. Do your best to move toward your goal. No one can know the outcome of a situation. Accept this while going the distance to complete your objective.

Fourth Line ▬▬ ▬▬

The more you practice the principles of the I Ching—patience, compassion, inner independence, strength, perseverance—the more your life will benefit. The better prepared you are for the marathon of life, the more likely you are to have a long and happy journey. Think of your teen years as the beginning of the marathon. Don't burn yourself out, and you will have what it takes for a long and happy life.

Running a Marathon

Fifth Line ━━━━ ━━━━

You started out awkwardly and poorly, but there is plenty of time to make up for this difficult start. Things will change for the better when you return to higher principles. Receiving this line can also be a reminder to keep to your commitments.

Sixth Line ━━━━━━━━━

Being modest, kind, and gentle does not mean that you have to be a pushover. The endurance it takes to finish a "marathon" is available only to those who don't give up. Reserve your energy for the final mile, and be careful not to be slowed down by questioning why things work out the way they do. Remain determined and focused, and you will succeed.

Consider

Richard Wilhelm and Cary F. Baynes give this hexagram the name of The Gentle (The Penetrating, Wind). Consider their comment on this hexagram: "Penetration produces gradual and inconspicuous effects. It should be effected not by an act of violation but by influence that never lapses. Results of this kind are less striking to the eye than those won by surprise attack, but they are more enduring and more complete. If one would produce such effects, one must have a clearly defined goal, for only when the penetrating influence works always in the same direction can the object be attained."

—Richard Wilhelm and Cary F. Baynes,
from *The I Ching or Book of Changes,* hexagram 57

Lake above

Lake below

58

The Art of Happiness

The happiness of our life depends on the quality of our thoughts.
—Marcus Aurelius Antoninus, Roman emperor

The I Ching teaches us that true and lasting happiness is obtained by those who live by higher principles. Acceptance is one such principle. This principle is about not always trying to change ourselves, others, or the situation. Instead, enter each moment with some openness to and acceptance of the situation and whatever it holds. Always wishing things were different or that we were older, or younger, or richer, or stronger generates a lot of unhappiness. Outward success is not a guarantee of happiness—stories of millionaire athletes arrested for drunk driving and famous actors who suffer from depression and loneliness are just two examples that prove happiness is not dependent on external factors.

Another principle that lends itself to happiness is inner independence, our ability to be free of others' opinions of us. When we get caught up in what we think others might think of us, we lose our perspective and our happiness. There isn't much we can do about other people's thoughts! Instead, we need to follow and respect our own Inner Truth, which will lead us to happiness and success.

Happiness comes to us because we have prepared the way for it. Receiving this hexagram implies that a time of happiness is at hand. Continue to apply the higher principles of acceptance and inner independence and your happiness will increase. A most happy outcome is indicated.

First Line ━━

The saying "want what you have" means that you should want what you already have and spend less time wanting more or wanting something else. Also, stop judging yourself harshly and comparing yourself with others. You are full of exceptional and wonderful qualities. Appreciation of who you are will bring about increased happiness.

Second Line ━━

Be true to yourself. Don't give up your beliefs just to go along with the crowd. If you practice inner independence you will achieve lasting happiness.

Third Line ━ ━

Giving in to drug abuse for a moment of fun will cause you to lose true and lasting joy. Be strong and independent, and happiness will follow. Drug abuse rapidly takes away your inner independence (because you come to depend on the drug) and your happiness (because it erodes your thoughts and well-being). Lasting happiness and joy are not dependent on material gain, getting high, or others.

Fourth Line ━━

You have been or are about to be tempted to do something that undermines true happiness. If you are undecided, wait until you know what it is you want before making a choice. It's often too easy to just let others make decisions for us, but to follow others now will not be a joyful experience in the end.

Fifth Line ━━━━

Someone may be trying to please you but is not being honest with you. There is danger in trusting others too quickly. Trust is something others need to attain from you over time. Find out the truth about the situation before moving forward with this person.

Sixth Line ━━ ━━

You are in a place of happiness. Now is the time to practice the higher principles and not lose sight of how these principles helped you to be so happy. What attitudes helped to bring you this happiness? How is this time of happiness related to inner qualities? Happiness tends to last longer when we reflect on how it was created.

Consider

Be involved in independent pastimes that bring you lasting happiness. Are you overly dependent on others to make you feel happy? Do you have to be in a relationship to feel good about yourself? Do you have to be successful on the outside or be recognized by others to be happy?

What brings you happiness from *within?* This does not mean that you shouldn't be in a relationship and that relationships don't make all of us happy—they do. But if you *can't* be happy when you are *not* in a relationship, long-lasting happiness will always escape you.

Find things that bring happiness to you, independent of others. Do you enjoy writing poetry or letters, meditating, reading, listening to music, making music, cooking, jogging, horseback riding, gardening, or tending an aquarium or raising another animal? Do more of these activities to increase your inner independence and your happiness. Learn to rely on yourself for some of your happiness.

Wind above

Water below

59

Forgiveness

In the autumn and winter, water begins to freeze into ice. When the warm breezes of spring come, the rigidity is dissolved, and the elements that have been dispersed in ice floes are reunited. It is the same with the minds of the people.
Richard Wilhelm and Cary F. Baynes,
from *The I Ching or Book of Changes*

The image associated with this hexagram is that of a warm spring wind blowing over ice and gradually melting it. It is time to "melt the ice," to remove any harshness that may exist within yourself or between you and someone else. The image of ice can represent rigidity, stubbornness, and judgmental attitudes that have become frozen in the mind or heart. Positive and creative energies are blocked by the ice of rigidity and other hard attitudes.

Receiving this hexagram means that it is time to break away the harshness and let the "ice" melt. Forgiveness is a universal icebreaker. Do you need to forgive yourself or someone else? Forgiveness has the ability to melt the hardest of feelings. To forgive means to "let go," to release. Forgiving someone can make it possible for you to have a relationship with this person, if you choose. To forgive means to let go of the need to punish yourself or others for some wrongdoing.

Once the ice is melted, pent-up energy is freed. Underneath the rigidity or stubbornness is creative and dynamic energy waiting to be released. So it is through the melting of hard feelings that you will now release these creative and positive energies and get things moving again.

Forgiving Others

We are often confused about what forgiveness is. We may want to be forgiving but feel confused and scared about what that might mean.

Forgiveness means

- "giving up" any negative emotions that you are holding on to;

- releasing hardened and blocked energy and thoughts;

- letting go of an offense or mistake so that it no longer has a harmful effect on you;

- processing the emotions that are keeping you connected to a particular person or event;

- allowing yourself to feel emotions;

- separating yourself from the behaviors of others;

- accepting yourself and others as fallible human beings;

- being present in the moment rather than reacting again and again to the past.

Forgiveness empowers you because the other person has less effect on you. Remember: forgiveness is a process that takes time, like melting ice.

Forgiveness does not mean

- appreciating or liking a particular individual;

- condoning the behavior of another person;

- forgetting.

You never have to be with anyone you don't want to be with, or of whom you are afraid. Forgiving someone does not mean that you have to spend any time with that person. You are not giving the person permission to repeat the offense/behavior when you forgive him or her. To forgive someone does not mean that that person is not to be punished or reprimanded for a harmful or illegal act. Forgiveness does not make you vulnerable to that person.

You do not have to "forgive all" in order to forgive. Give up whatever you decide you have held on to for too long.

First Line ▬▬ ▬▬

You are becoming stubborn due to a misunderstanding. Take some steps now to open up and communicate with this person. Remember: understanding someone does not necessarily mean that you agree (hexagram 38). You can fully understand someone and still disagree.

Second Line ▬▬▬▬

You are feeling alienated and shut out by others. To improve the situation you need to do something to "melt the ice." This may mean approaching them with an open heart and mind or changing your attitude.

Third Line ▬▬ ▬▬

To succeed now depends entirely on you breaking free from any hostile feelings you have held on to until now.

Fourth Line ▬▬ ▬▬

Work toward the happiness and well-being of everyone concerned and you will be pleased with the result. If you consider only yourself, disappointment will result. The following prayer may help you be considerate of others.

I pray for the best possible outcome for all concerned.

Repeat this prayer every time you are worried about the outcome of a situation.

Fifth Line ▬▬

The best response to the difficulty at hand is to pull people together for a common cause or celebration.

Sixth Line ▬▬

Stop focusing on negative feelings and concerns. The I Ching encourages a neutral approach to difficulty, which means an acceptance of the situation without doing anything against your principles. Distance yourself from the trouble.

Consider

What might be good icebreakers? Forgiveness can be one. But sometimes we need to break up frozen energy and attitudes by *moving*. Prayer, drumming, dancing, chanting, singing, and group meditations and rituals can break up hardened energy. These activities can invite forth the creative and dynamic energy that is blocked.

An Icebreaker

No matter how down or stuck you feel, movement will always help you feel better. Following is a simple way to start melting the ice. You will need paper, your favorite CDs, and paint (finger paint would be great!), magic markers, or watercolor pens.

Find four of your favorite tunes that are great to dance to. Get out a large piece of paper and some paints (or watercolor pens or magic markers). Play the first song and sing aloud with it. Then, play the second song, and starting with the bottom of your legs, and moving upward, gently pat your entire body. Pat your legs, torso, buttocks, sides, back, arms, hands, neck, face, and head. Pat gently, but hard enough to get the blood flowing. Then dance to the third song. Finally, when playing the fourth song, paint something fast and furious without stopping. Paint with the music. When the music stops, stop painting.

When finished, go for at least a half-hour walk. Ask a friend to meet you somewhere, if you like. Notice how you feel in your body. Notice what your emotions are and your change in thoughts.

Water above

Lake below

60

Reasonable Limits

He who cannot obey himself will be commanded.
This is the nature of living creatures.
—Friedrich Nietzsche, nineteenth-century German philosopher and poet

Whereas "the sky's the limit," we don't want to be like Icarus, who forgot his limits and flew too close to the sun. He had the entire heavens to fly in (as you do), but this too had its limits. He and his father were imprisoned, so Icarus made wings to escape, which he did successfully. However, he ignored his father's warning and flew too close to the sun, and the wings, made of wax, melted. In receiving this hexagram, you are being warned to pay attention to limits and boundaries.

As the opening quote states, if we don't limit ourselves, circumstances or others will. When we respect the natural limits, we find we can achieve a great many things. During our teen years sometimes we feel too limited, while other times we

are busting through all limits! We are like Icarus, escaping at times what imprisons us, so we have to be aware of our limits and the limits of our environment.

In every relationship and experience there are natural boundaries that need to be respected: teachers cannot have sex with their students; if we ride bikes and hit our heads on the cement, we harm our heads; we can die from drinking too much alcohol or mixing drugs and alcohol. Respecting such limits and boundaries creates safe experiences for each of us.

The teen years are a natural time to push the limits. Push the limits, but keep in mind that there are still boundaries that we need to respect. A life without acknowledgment of boundaries can be destructive and confusing. Limits and boundaries actually help us define what we are willing to do and what we are not willing to do. This hexagram may mean that you are testing your limits or that someone else is trying to cross a line with you. Be warned, and take care. Fly high, fly very high, but respect the heat and danger of the sun.

First Line ━━━

You have your mind set on a certain goal, but you are still being limited. Be careful what you say and do at this time. This is not the time to push against the limit that is being imposed upon you. Learn instead to accept that there are such times of limitation.

Second Line ━━━

Don't restrict yourself with unreasonable limits. You are afraid of something and are holding yourself back. This is the time to take action, to seize the moment.

Third Line ━━ ━━

Stop blaming others, and take responsibility for your own choices and behaviors.

Fourth Line ━━ ━━

Learn to notice when others are receptive to you: this is when the door is open to you and is a time of possibility. Likewise, learn to notice when others are not receptive to you and the opportunity is closed. This is a very helpful skill, one that allows you to quickly assess when to act and when not to. To learn such a limit is a great skill to have throughout your life. If those around you are not receptive at this time, back off. An opening will return.

Fifth Line ━━━━━

This is a time of opportunity. Go ahead and take advantage of the situation. How you handle this moment of opportunity affects how others will relate to you. This line also means that you need to practice what you preach. You need to live by the limits you impose on others.

Sixth Line ━━ ━━

Don't be too rigid in setting limits for yourself or others. Be receptive to change. Be kind and patient with yourself and others as you learn the value of natural limits.

Sitting on Top of the Great Mountain Exercise

To get a sense of where you are now, take a moment and imagine yourself on top of a great mountain. You are far above everything and can see for great distances in all directions. Use this great vision to see your life, to gain more perspective.

Behind you is your life so far . . . all that has come to pass up to this moment. What do you see? What events brought you to this place in your life? What choices did you or others make that determined your life so far? How have you used this time? Can you see how one choice leads into another? What losses, trauma, or pain have you suffered? How have these affected you? What gifts, happiness, and opportunities have been given to you so far? Notice how all this has led you to YOUR LIFE NOW.

To your sides is your life now. Who are your friends? What do you give your time to? What pain are you experiencing? What gifts and opportunities are being offered to you now? What choices are you making that will determine what is to come? What are your dreams and fears? What problems and challenges face your community and the planet at this time?

In front of you is your future. What do you see? When you look in this direction it stretches out further, beyond all that you can see. But what awaits you in the near future, because of how you are living now? What do you see awaiting you and the planet in the distant future if you continue to go on as you are presently? Can you easily imagine that the future side of the mountain is vast and expansive, meaning there are many possibilities out there for you?

Now take a few moments to write down your thoughts, feelings, and responses to this exercise. Date it, so you can reflect on it later. After you have consulted the I Ching a few more times, return to this exercise and experience it again. Now, what do you see as you sit on top of the great mountain?

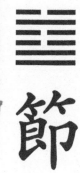

Voluntary chosen limits empower your growth.

—**Brian Browne Walker,**
from ***The I Ching or Book of Changes,*** hexagram 60

Wind above

Lake below

61

Trusting Your Intuition

It is not simply a matter of blindly following the oracle, but rather of understanding one's place within the situation.
—Taoist Master Alfred Huang, from *The Complete I Ching*

To understand our place in a situation we must be able to hear and trust our inner wisdom, our intuition. No matter how beautiful and wise someone else's advice may be, *always follow your own truth*. In Tibetan Buddhism, the adage "Of the two witnesses, trust the principle one" means, when given two points of view, trust your intuition and Inner Truth above all else. Always move toward your own truth. When we are in conflict and weighing many possibilities, it is important to go within and find what we feel to be right and true, especially when it comes to ourselves.

It can be difficult at times to let go of what we think others want from us. It helps to take our focus off others and return to our Inner Truth. It is often quite difficult to

take our minds off others, what they are doing (or not doing), and what we think they may be thinking! The peace and answers we seek, however, come to us from knowing *ourselves*. To come to a wise and correct decision requires us to look within for the truth. This doesn't mean we should ignore all advice, but we need to use our intuition to weigh others' suggestions.

In following the guidance of the I Ching don't follow it blindly; consider how it applies to your life now, in this situation. Take the time to contemplate its meaning for you.

First Line ━━━━

You were born with the ability to use your inner wisdom and tap in to your intuitive powers. Identify what habits of thought and behaviors have kept you from tapping in to this resource. Are you too hard on yourself, or doubtful? Do you abuse drugs or alcohol? Do you not trust what your "gut" tells you, because you are afraid to follow its nudges? Do you hang out with those who belittle you and your intuition? Find what gets in the way of this incredible power you have, and work at removing these obstacles.

Second Line ━━━━

Your attitude is always communicated to others (even when you don't say anything). If you are committed to good things, other people will feel this; if you hold on to negative attitudes, people will feel this too.
This line also refers to the company you keep and how it influences you. Are you surrounding yourself with those who empower you or belittle you? Those who empower you will help you trust your intuition and Inner Truth.

Third Line ━━ ━━

This line warns you not to depend too much on others in order to feel good about yourself and not to follow someone else's advice if your intuition warns you against this. If you constantly seek the approval of others, then you will not be able to hear the guidance of your intuition.

Fourth Line ━━ ━━

Recognizing your dependence on a Higher Power brings good results. Your Inner Truth and Higher Power are connected. In fact, the Higher Power communicates with you through your intuition.

Fifth Line ━━━━

Your ability to change your attitude from a negative one to a positive one brings good to what was once a difficult relationship. Continue to have a good attitude, and others will listen to you.

Sixth Line ━━━━

You have gained insight and access to your intuition through reflection and meditation. You've come to understand an important truth about the situation. Trust what you know. However, don't force this truth on others. Everyone comes to the truth in his or her own way and in his or her own time.

Consider

Build your intuition by practicing the following exercise as often as possible.

For a time (until it becomes a habit), ask yourself, "What am I *feeling?*" "What am I *thinking?*" "What do I *want?*" Simply check in with yourself, especially during times of confusion. Don't force any answer, just open yourself to the response. Simply asking yourself these questions will bring on intuitive wisdom. If you keep asking yourself, "What am I feeling?" you will get insight into what it is you are feeling. So don't forget to check in with yourself—feelings, thoughts, and desires are a direct link to the intuition.

In order for us to feel our wholeness, we need to live
creatively and open up fully to our intuition.

**—Colleen Brenzy,
intuitive healer, philosopher**

Thunder above

Mountain below

62

Small Steps

Nothing great is created suddenly, any more than a bunch of grapes or a fig.
—Epictetus, ancient Greek Stoic philosopher

Too many people spend money they haven't earned, to buy things they don't want, to impress people they don't like.
—Will Rogers, American actor and humorist

This is the time to give your attention to small things, to details. It is also a time to take small steps. Attend to your immediate needs, and don't overextend yourself in any way just to impress others. Make no great changes in plans at this time. It would be better to do less than to do too much. Find the value in the small steps that are necessary here. What is the next step you need to take in order to move toward

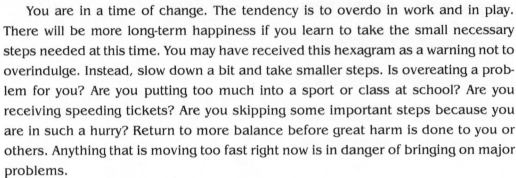

your goal? A "bunch of grapes" doesn't become so overnight, and what you are wanting to accomplish requires many small steps as well.

You are in a time of change. The tendency is to overdo in work and in play. There will be more long-term happiness if you learn to take the small necessary steps needed at this time. You may have received this hexagram as a warning not to overindulge. Instead, slow down a bit and take smaller steps. Is overeating a problem for you? Are you putting too much into a sport or class at school? Are you receiving speeding tickets? Are you skipping some important steps because you are in such a hurry? Return to more balance before great harm is done to you or others. Anything that is moving too fast right now is in danger of bringing on major problems.

Also, when meeting new people, be aware of the small but necessary steps needed to establish a truly caring relationship.

First Line ▬ ▬

Do not exceed your limits. Don't bite off more than you can chew (or if you have, stop now). Take the time and steps needed to gain more understanding of the situation.

Second Line ▬ ▬

Get help from an adult you respect. There is not much else you can do until you receive some help. All will go well if you succeed in reaching out.

Third Line ▬▬▬

You are acting correctly, but there are those around you who do not hold your best interest in mind. Be careful in your relationships. Take your time, and do what you know is the right thing.

Fourth Line ▬▬▬

Things are going well, and you are practicing the Higher Principles suggested in the I Ching. Don't let this success turn into arrogance or righteousness. Keep your steps small and humble.

Fifth Line ━ ━

You have the right ideas and concerns in mind, but the time is not right to act. Prepare the way for yourself by fostering your attention to detail.

Sixth Line ━ ━

You will experience trouble if you go beyond your means. Something at this time remains beyond your grasp.

Walking Meditation

Give yourself about ten to fifteen minutes to practice this popular meditation. You can be outside or inside for this meditation.

Begin to walk, and bring your attention to your walking. Simply be aware of your body moving, your legs walking . . . Now slow it down. Bring your attention to your body as it moves. Begin noticing your body and the physical sensations of walking. Now slow it down even more . . . Notice that as you slow down it is easier to be aware of your walking. Slow down enough to notice your feet rising from the ground and landing, one step at a time. When your thoughts wander, with great kindness return your awareness to the walking. Do this for at least five minutes.

Now walk a bit more, feeling gratitude for your ability to walk. Remember that there are many people bound to wheelchairs or beds. We often take for granted our ability to move about freely, and slowing down allows us to appreciate our bodies and our good fortune.

For more on walking meditations and other mindfulness meditations you may want to read *Wherever You Go, There You Are: Mindfulness Meditation in Everyday Life* by Jon Kabat-Zinn (New York: Hyperion, 1994).

Water above

Fire below

63

Fulfillment

God
Disguised
As myriad things and
Playing a game
Of tag

Has kissed you and said,
"You're it—

I mean, you're Really IT!

Now
It does not matter
What you believe or feel
For something wonderful,

Major-league Wonderful
Is someday going
      To

Happen.
—Hafiz, Sufi master, from ***The Gift: Poems by Hafiz***

This is a time of fulfillment. Everything is as it should be. You have accomplished something that you have worked toward. This is a time of harmony, balance; everything is working together. It's an ideal time for you. The I Ching advises you to use this time wisely and to know that good times, too, come to an end.

Because you are in a state of fulfillment, remember to keep true to your spiritual principles. Sometimes when we are experiencing such great times, we forget how we got here and become too complacent. Similar to the time of graduation, it is a time to enjoy and acknowledge your accomplishments. But remain focused on your path and where you hope to go next.

You can use this time of fulfillment to guide you further through your teen years by considering the questions in the box on page 218. What is it you hope to accomplish or experience next in your life? Are you needing to do things that further help prepare you for your adult years, when you will be on your own? What might this include? Receiving this hexagram indicates that it is an ideal time to prepare for the future. When you have prepared well great times approach.

First Line ━━━

This is a time of caution and progress. If you are careful at the beginning of a project or relationship, it will lead to a happy outcome.

Second Line ━━ ━━

A small and temporary delay is preventing you from moving forward. Don't push it. Wait out this delay, and when the time is right things will begin moving again.

Third Line ━━━

The success that is coming your way has not been easy to obtain. It is still important to be careful and focus on your plans for the future. This line reminds you that your plans and goals affect other people, and you must take them into account.

Fourth Line — —

Others may have hidden agendas (secret intentions) that cause you trouble. Or, you may hold secret resentments about others. Practice tolerance of other people's wrongdoing and find a way to let go of your resentment. Receiving this line may also mean you have asked someone to help you who is not reliable. Let them go.

Fifth Line ——

You have or are about to achieve a goal. Acknowledge the help of others and the Higher Power that made this success possible. Enjoy the success, and share your happiness with others.

Sixth Line — —

You have come to the end of some project or relationship. Everything in life changes. Now is the time to prepare for a new beginning.

Consider

What are your plans after you finish high school or college? Travel abroad, get more education, start that job, move to a different city? Do you have a larger picture of what you want to accomplish in your lifetime? Do you hold in your heart a purpose? Even though these ideas can change, this is a good time to consider your dreams, plans, and purpose. What passions do you hold? Answering these questions will help move you deliberately toward your future, as your future moves toward you.

Life is a series of surprises.

—Ralph Waldo Emerson,
American essayist, poet, and spiritual philosopher

64

Change Is the Rule of Life

Behind the night . . . somewhere afar
Some white tremendous daybreak.
—Rupert Brooke, English poet

This is the beginning of a new cycle. This hexagram is the final one, which reminds us that every time something ends, a new beginning follows. At such times feelings of doubt and confusion sometimes arise. We become worried about what the future holds. Stay grounded in the truth that you are in the natural cycle of change and life, moving from completion to beginning again. In reality, we need to begin again every day. Every day has its beginning, middle, and end. Our lives are a series of beginnings, middles, and ends as well. Where are you in the cycle of what you're inquiring

about? Are you trying to skip the middle and get right to the end? Notice how endings in the past have led to new things—new beginnings.

This transition through the teen years can feel like the dark before the dawn, but remember that the dawn always comes. Daybreak is near. You feel this doubt because you don't have a full sense of what the next development is. Don't fill this time of darkness (which is coming to an end) with doubt. Rest in the wisdom of truth. Just as darkness gives way to the new dawn, your confusion and doubt will give way to a time of understanding and fulfillment. This time is rich with potential.

In many ways, the teen years are similar to the cycle of the days—this is the time right before the dawn of your adult independence, the dawn of your adult life. The potential of this time in life is intense and unceasing. Know that the dawn will come soon and that what you do in the last years of "darkness" before this dawn will influence the rest of your life.

First Line ▬ ▬

Don't act hastily. You have a good sense of what you want to do but not a complete enough picture (dawn hasn't arrived yet) to act. When light is shed on the situation (you obtain the bigger picture), you will know what to do.

Second Line ▬▬▬

This is the time to be exceedingly careful. An opportunity is approaching, but the time is not right yet. Be patient. Wait for the sun to rise.

Third Line ▬ ▬

Do not let others rush your decision. Take the time to think things through for yourself. You will make the right choice on your own.

Fourth Line ▬▬▬

You will make great progress if you don't allow the situation or others to throw you off balance. Sometimes the dark before the dawn feels as if it will never end, so we try to come up with quick solutions. Rest assured that the light is approaching, and the difficulty will pass. Keep your inner independence, and success will follow.

Fifth Line — —

You have made it! You're on your way! Practicing the principles of patience and inner independence has paid off.

Sixth Line ———

When success comes, as it has for you, maintain inner independence and tolerance of those who do not understand the spiritual path you have chosen. Do not lose self-control during times of success, and the happiness will last longer.

Consider

The I Ching teaches us to take the middle road and not to get so caught up in the drama of life. We are too often thrown off course by events—today a "great event," tomorrow an "awful event." We feel something is "great" or "awful," not realizing the limits of those times. Do you know anyone (or yourself, perhaps) who is always involved or caught up in some big drama? In his book *The Four Agreements,* don Miguel Ruiz speaks much on the value of getting out of the drama cycle, where we perpetuate unnecessary difficulty. Life is never all good or all bad—it is a mix, and most important, **it is always changing.** Good times can't last forever, but neither will the negative times. Consider the following story and its meaning. How do finding and accepting a middle path help us move with change?

Once upon a time there was a very old Chinese farmer. He lived on his farm with his son and a horse. Without them he would never have been able to manage the farm. Respected by people from miles around, he was known as a wise man, and when people needed help or advice, they would seek him out. One day the old man's horse ran away and didn't return. The man and his son searched high and low for the horse, but they couldn't find it. It had seemingly vanished into thin air.

When the neighbors found out about the horse's disappearance, they came to see the old man and console him. "Old man," they said, "we're really sorry to hear about your horse running away. What are you going to do? You need the horse to work your farm. What bad news!" The old man looked at them and said, "Good news, bad news. Who knows?"

The neighbors didn't know what to make of that answer, but the old man refused to say more and so they left. A couple of days later they heard that the old man's horse had come back and brought a wild horse with it. Now the old man had two horses. Well, the neighbors were so happy for the old man they were back at his place the next day telling him, "Old man, we're so glad to hear about your good news. Now you have two horses." The old man looked at them and said, "Good news, bad news. Who knows?"

The neighbors didn't know what to make of the old man. They had a lot of respect for him, but they didn't understand why he wasn't happy and excited with this unexpected stroke of good fortune.

The next day they heard that the old man's son was trying to break the wild horse when he fell from the horse and broke his leg. The neighbors converged on the old man's farm. They were adamant. "Old man," they said, "surely now you must admit that this is bad luck. This is your son we're talking about. How are you going to take care of him and take care of your farm? You are dependent on him. Certainly this is terrible bad news." But the old man just looked at them with a light smile on his face. "Good news, bad news. Who knows?"

The neighbors were frustrated. They didn't understand the old man. They went back to their homes, only to have the army came through the area the next day, taking all able-bodied young men to fight in a terrible war. The parents of these young men were devastated. They knew many of their sons would not return. Of course, the army couldn't take the old man's son because he had a broken leg. The neighbors were overjoyed. They rushed back to the old man's house.

"Old man," they said, "surely you must admit that this is good news." But the old man looked at them and said, "Won't you ever learn? Good news, bad news. Who knows?"

Bibliography for Further Exploration into the I Ching

Book of Changes: Poems, by Karen Holden, North Atlantic Books, 1998.

The Buddhist I Ching: Chih-hsu Ou-I, translated by Thomas Cleary., Shambhala Publications, 1987.

The Complete I Ching: The Definitive Translation, by Taoist Master Alfred Huang, Inner Traditions, 1998.

The Encyclopedia of Eastern Philosophy and Religion, edited by Stephan Schuhmacher and Gert Woerner, Shambhala Publications, 1986.

Essential Changes: The Essence of the I Ching, translated by Daniel Lomax, Omen Press, 1972.

Shambhala: The Sacred Path of the Warrior, by Chögyam Trungpa, Shambhala Publications, 1984.

Starting Where You Are: A Guide To Compassionate Living, by Pema Chödrön, Shambhala Publications, 1994.

A Gradual Awakening, by Stephen Levine, Doubleday, 1989.

The I Ching or Book of Changes, translated from Chinese to German by Richard Wilhelm and translated into English by Cary F. Baynes, Third Edition, Princeton University Press, 1967.

The I Ching or Book of Changes: A Guide to Life's Turning Points, by Brian Browne Walker, St. Martin's Press, 1992.

A New Interpretation For Modern Times: I Ching, translated by Sam Reifler, Bantam Books, 1974.

The Philosophy of the I Ching, by Carol K. Anthony, Anthony Publishing, 1981.

The Tao of Psychology: Synchronicity and the Self, by Jean Shinoda Bolen, M.D., Harper & Row, 1979.

The Taoist I Ching, translated by Thomas Cleary, Shambhala Publications, 1986.

Zen Mind, Beginner's Mind, by Shunryu Suzuki, Weatherhill, 1991.

Zen Soup: Tasty Morsels of Wisdom from Great Minds East and West, by Laurence G. Boldt, Penguin, 1997.

Identifying Your Hexagram

TRIGRAMS								
UPPER ▶	CH'IEN	CH'ÊN	K'AN	KÊN	K'UN	SUN	LI	TUI
LOWER ▼	Heaven	Thunder	Water	Mountain	Earth	Wind	Fire	Lake
CH'IEN / Heaven	1	34	5	26	11	9	14	43
CH'ÊN / Thunder	25	51	3	27	24	42	21	17
K'AN / Water	6	40	29	4	7	59	64	47
KÊN / Mountain	33	62	39	52	15	53	56	31
K'UN / Earth	12	16	8	23	2	20	35	45
SUN / Wind	44	32	48	18	46	57	50	28
LI / Fire	13	55	63	22	36	37	30	49
TUI / Lake	10	54	60	41	19	61	38	58

Origins

We are exploding stars—with a center still intact. Some particles are hell-bent for going out farther and farther. Others remember/imagine the old pull of gravity and want to fall back to earth—into mother's lap. Always *this* pull against *that* one. Pulls two into one, into two, into one into two . . . blossoms into multitudes.

— Shannon King, American poet